To Taylor
Hope you enjoy the book
Robert E Hollman

Frontier Legends

presents

Susannah Dickinson

by

Robert E. Hollman

Durban House

Printed in the United States of America.

For information address:
Durban House Press, Inc.
7502 Greenville Avenue, Suite 500, Dallas, Texas 75231

Library of Congress Cataloging-in-Publication Data

Hollmann, Robert E., 1944 -

Susannah Dickinson / Robert E. Hollmann

Library of Congress Control Number: 2007929257

p. cm.

ISBN: 0-9779863-3-0

First Edition

10 9 8 7 6 5 4 3 2 1

Visit our Web site at
http://www.durbanhouse.com

To all the little girls who believe that dolls can talk.

Acknowledgments

Many people gave me encouragement to write this book. I appreciate all of them. I want to thank the Daughters of the Republic of Texas Library for allowing me to use the picture of Susannah Dickinson on the cover. I want to thank my publisher, John Lewis, and his wife, Karen, for all they do to promote this series. As always, my family has supported me in this effort, especially my wife, Kathy, who told me that dolls really could talk.

Robert E. Hollmann
Odessa, Texas
November 2006

Chapter One

THE OLD ATTIC WAS DARK. Only a slender moonbeam that shone through a small window disturbed the darkness. Spider webs hung from the ceiling, and dust covered the old furniture that had been placed in the attic for storage. A mouse scurried through the furniture. When it disappeared into a hole in the wall, nothing else moved.

A group of toys lay on the attic floor. In an old rocking chair, a rag doll stared at the darkness through button eyes. The yellow yarn that made her hair was unraveling. Her red-and-white-checked dress was faded and stained. One of her knees had a tear in it, and stuffing poked through the hole. Still, you could tell that at one time this doll had been pretty. She had been some little girl's best friend.

The grandfather clock downstairs in the living room

began to chime. When the last chime struck midnight, a change came over the attic. A ballerina doll got slowly to her feet. She stood on her toes and walked around the attic.

"Wake up, everybody," she called softly. "It's midnight. Time to wake up and play."

The rocking horse began to rock back and forth. "Anybody want a ride?"

The jack-in-the-box popped up. "Not me, thanks. I fell off the last time I rode you."

The ballerina doll continued to walk around the attic. Finally she stopped in front of a tin soldier.

"Hello. You must be new. I don't remember seeing you here before."

The tin soldier held his gun and looked around. "Yes, I just got here today. The boy who used to play with me has grown up, so they put me up here with all of you."

The ballerina doll smiled. "Yes, it happens to all of us. Our children grow up and no longer play with us. They move on to other things. You're welcome here. Every night at midnight we come to life. We can stay alive until the sun comes up. We have fun here. We play and sometimes we tell stories."

The tin soldier laughed. "I can just imagine the stories a bunch of broken old toys would tell. I used to fight in battles with my little boy. We never lost. We didn't do silly things like the rest of you did."

A teddy bear with one ear missing looked at the tin soldier. "Silly things! We made our children happy. I don't think you can call that silly."

The tin soldier shook his head. "We used to build forts, cross rivers, and attack castles. We played war all the time. We didn't dance around on our toes or rock back and forth in one place all day. I can't believe I ended up here with all you boring old toys."

The ballerina doll smiled at the tin soldier. "You like stories about battles? We have someone here who was in a real battle. Not one of your play ones. You should talk to her if you want to know about battles."

"Her?" The tin soldier laughed. "Are you telling me a doll was in a real battle? I don't believe you."

The ballerina doll turned and started to walk away. "Come with me."

The ballerina walked a few steps then turned to see if the tin soldier was following. He stood there looking at her.

"Come on," she said. "Don't be afraid. It's after midnight. You can walk now."

"I'm not afraid of anything. Certainly not of you broken old toys."

The ballerina doll led him to the old rocking chair. The other toys followed and soon they were standing all around the chair. The ballerina doll looked at the rag doll sitting above her.

"Hello, Patty," she said. "We have a new toy." She pointed to the tin soldier who was standing next to her.

The rag doll looked at the tin soldier. "Hello. Nice to have you with us."

"Patty," the ballerina doll said. "The tin soldier used to play like he was fighting battles. I told him that you were in a real battle once. Would you tell him the story?"

Patty looked at the tin soldier. "He looks very brave. I'm sure he doesn't want to hear my story."

The tin soldier looked at Patty. "What battle were you in?"

"The battle of the Alamo."

The tin soldier laughed. "You were at the Alamo? Now I know you're teasing me. I've heard of Colonel Travis and Jim Bowie and Davy Crockett. But I've never heard of a rag doll being at the Alamo."

The rag doll smiled. "Yes, all of those men were at the Alamo. I knew them and many others. I was there. I saw the battle from the first day to the last. Would you like for me to tell you about it?"

The tin soldier nodded. "Sure. Tell me about it. Tell me how a rag doll ended up at the battle of the Alamo."

The rag doll motioned for all of the toys to sit down. "All right. I'll tell you the story of the Alamo, but first I'm going to tell you the story of a very special friend of mine. A lady who was with me at the Alamo. A lady who shared her life with me for many years. I'm going to tell you the story of Susannah Dickinson."

Chapter Two

THE STORY STARTED A LONG TIME AGO. I was sitting on a shelf in a general store in a small town in Tennessee. All day I would watch the people come in and out of the store. Sometimes little girls would come and look at me. Some even held me, but every time their mothers made them put me back on the shelf. I was beginning to think I would never leave the store.

One day the door opened and a woman walked in with her young daughter. The girl was pretty. She had dark hair and blue eyes.

"Good morning, Mrs. Wilkerson," the store owner said. "What can I do for you today?"

While Mrs. Wilkerson gave her order to the man, the young girl walked around the store. I watched her as she looked at the jars of candy. She felt some new cloth that had just arrived. At last she saw me and walked over. She looked at me for a while and then lifted me off the shelf. She walked around the store holding me. I liked the way she held me. I hoped I could go home with her.

"Susannah," her mother called. "Come on. We must go home. Put the doll back."

I didn't want to stay in the store. My arms were draped over her neck. I wished I could grab tighter. I thought that if she put me back I would cry, even though I knew I couldn't.

"Oh, Mama," Susannah said. "Let me have her. I think she is the prettiest doll I've ever seen."

"No, dear. We can't afford that doll. Put it back."

Susannah started to walk toward the shelf. She wanted to keep me and I wanted to go with her, but it seemed we had to part.

"Mrs. Wilkerson," the owner said. "I've had that doll for awhile. It's been handled quite a bit. I can't really call it new. I will make you a good price on it. You're a good customer and I can see that your daughter wants it very badly."

Susannah stopped and clasped me to her. She looked at her mother with her big blue eyes. Mrs. Wilkerson stared at us, then gave a sigh.

"Oh, all right. Put it on my bill. I think it's an ugly doll, but Susannah seems to like it. Come on now. We must get home."

As Susannah carried me out of that store, I was the happiest doll in the whole world. We climbed on the wagon and soon were heading for my new home.

The next few years were very happy for Susannah and me. We became the greatest of friends. She took me everywhere. At night we slept in her bed under the soft quilts her mother made. In the woods in back of the cabin,

Susannah made a hideaway. We played many games there. Some days we would have tea parties. Other days the hideaway would be a castle and we would be princesses. We never ran out of things to do in our secret place.

Susannah was growing up, and soon we stopped going to the hideaway, but she still took me with her. Even if she had to go to school, I would go with her and sit with her coat until she could go home. As she grew older and prettier, the boys began to hang around her. Sometimes they would try to take me away from her, but she would hit them and chase them away.

One day as we walked home from school, we passed a blacksmith shop. A young man was hammering on a horseshoe as we passed. Susannah looked at him and smiled as we walked by. The young man wiped his forehead and waved to us. I thought he was good looking. I looked up at Susannah and I could tell she thought so too.

Every day after school we would walk by the blacksmith shop, and every day the young man would be there. We found out that the young man's name was Almeron Dickinson.

One day we stopped and talked to him. He was nice, and soon Susannah and Almeron were taking walks together and going on picnics. Of course I went too. Even though she was fifteen, Susannah always took me with her. One day as we sat under a tree, Almeron picked me up.

"Why do you take this doll everywhere you go?"

Susannah took me from Almeron and gave me a hug. "Patty is a special friend of mine. We've been together for a long time. If she were alive, she would be my sister."

Almeron laughed. "Well, it's good to have a friend."

Things were going well. Then one day Almeron and

Susannah got into an argument. I can't remember what the argument was about. I just remember lying in bed with Susannah that night. I remember how soft and warm the quilt was. She turned to me and I saw tears run down her cheeks. She hugged me and I felt her tears on my face. "I'll tell you one thing, Patty," she said. "I never want to see Almeron Dickinson again."

Chapter Three

THE DAYS FOLLOWING SUSANNAH'S BREAKUP with Almeron were not pleasant ones. Susannah was quiet and sometimes left me on the bed while she walked in the woods. I guess she needed to be alone, but I missed the walks with her. Finally she began to take me with her again. It seemed that no matter where we walked, we always ended up walking by the blacksmith's shop. Almeron was always there working. He would look up as we passed by. Susannah would look away, but I could tell by the hurt in her eyes that she wanted to stop and talk with him. Almeron looked the same way, but he would beat on the horseshoe he was working on like he never noticed us. I swear sometimes humans can be as stubborn as mules.

One day we heard that Almeron was seeing Josie Martin. Josie was friends with Susannah. When Susannah heard this, she became quiet again. She went back to walking in the woods, but this time she took me.

One day we had just returned from one of our walks. We were sitting in front of our cabin and Susannah was braiding my hair. We looked down the road and saw Josie walking toward us. She was skipping and humming a song. It was easy to see that she was happy. Soon she stood in front of us.

"Hello, Susannah," she said.

Susannah continued to braid my hair. "Hello, Josie. What brings you over here?"

Josie smiled. "I have the best news. Almeron and I are getting married."

Susannah nearly dropped me. "Getting married? When?"

"In a few weeks. We already talked to the preacher. He's going to announce it in church Sunday. Be sure to be there."

Susannah didn't say anything. She gripped me so tight that I thought my stuffing would come out. Josie twirled around.

"My mother's making me a dress. You should see it. It's blue and white, and I'm going to wear flowers in my hair. Oh, I really can't wait."

"I'm sure your dress will be real pretty," Susannah said. She started to get up.

"Wait," Josie said. She reached down and put her hand on Susannah's shoulder. "I want you to be one of my bridesmaids."

I could see the shock come onto Susannah's face. Once more I feared for my stuffing. Susannah opened her mouth but nothing came out.

"Please say you will," Josie begged. "Please, please."

"I don't know," Susannah said. "I don't really have anything to wear."

"You have time to get a dress. The general store just got in some new cloth. Your mother is a great seamstress. Why, she can make you a dress in no time. Pick out some light blue cloth. That's what I'm asking all my bridesmaids to do. Will you do this, Susannah?"

Susannah looked down at me. I could tell she felt like she was trapped. She looked back at Josie.

"Of course. I'll be happy to."

Josie bent down and hugged Susannah's neck. "Thank you, Susannah. This will be so much fun. I'll talk to you later. I need to go ask some other girls to be in the wedding."

We watched Josie go skipping happily down the road. Susannah held me in her arms. Suddenly I felt a teardrop fall on my face. I looked up and saw tears running down Susannah's cheeks. She didn't say a word. She just turned and walked inside the cabin.

The next few weeks were filled with plans for the wedding. Josie came by often and talked about it all the time. Susannah's mother worked on her dress and soon it was ready for her to try on. She looked pretty in the dress. I thought she should be the bride.

One night shortly before the wedding, Susannah got out of her bed and put her new dress on. She picked me up and we slipped quietly out of the house. She didn't say a word as we walked through the darkened town. I had no idea where we were going. Soon we stopped in front of the house where Almeron was living. Susannah walked around to the room where he slept and tapped on the window.

Almeron opened the window and looked out.

"Susannah. What are you doing here at this hour?" he asked.

"I want to talk to you," she said. "Come out here."

Almeron yawned and rubbed his eyes. "Talk to me? Now? Let's talk tomorrow."

He pulled his head in and started to close the window. Susannah stuck her hand through the window and grabbed his nightshirt.

"Almeron Dickinson, you come out here right now."

Almeron looked at Susannah. He nodded his head. "All right. Let me get dressed. I'll meet you in back in five minutes."

In a short period of time Almeron met us in back of the house. I watched him walk slowly toward us.

"All right, Susannah. What's so important it won't wait until morning?"

"Almeron Dickinson, what do you mean marrying Josie Martin?"

"Why, I guess that's my business," he said.

"It's not just your business. You never asked me."

"I don't guess I need to ask you if I can marry Josie," Almeron said.

"Not ask me that. You never asked me to marry you."

Almeron and I were both shocked at that statement. I could tell he didn't know what to say. Finally he shrugged his shoulders and said, "You wouldn't even talk to me. I thought you couldn't stand me. Why would I ask somebody like that to marry me?"

"Well, you were wrong. I can stand you. If you had any sense you'd know that."

Almeron stood there shaking his head. "You mean if I asked you to marry me, you'd say yes?"

"Try it and see," Susannah said.

Almeron looked at me, but I didn't say anything. I was as surprised as he was. He took a deep breath. "All right, Susannah. Will you marry me?"

Susannah nodded her head. "Yes I will. Thank you for asking."

Almeron still had a look of disbelief on his face. "You will? But I'm marrying Josie."

"Not for another week," Susannah said.

"When do you want us to get married?" he asked.

"We can wake up the justice of the peace and get married tonight," she said.

"Tonight? Don't you need to get ready?"

"I have on my new dress. Patty can be my bridesmaid. Are you ready or not?"

A smile crossed Almeron's face. "I'm ready."

A short while later Almeron paid the sleepy justice of the peace, and Mr. and Mrs. Almeron Dickinson walked out into the early morning light.

"Well, Almeron," Susannah said. "Since I'm now your wife, I need to know what your plans are."

Almeron put his arm on her shoulder. "I've been thinking about moving on. I guess this would be as good a time as any."

Susannah looked at her new husband. "Moving on? Where are we going?"

Almeron gave her shoulder a squeeze. "We're going to a place I heard about where land is plentiful and cheap. Where a man can start a new life and make a good home for his family."

"It sounds nice," Susannah said. "What's this place called?"

Almeron looked toward the west and smiled. "It has a nice-sounding name. It's called Texas."

Chapter Four

I HAD NO IDEA HOW BIG TEXAS WAS. It seemed that we had been traveling forever. We joined with some other settlers for the trip. This made me feel better because I had heard stories about the Comanche Indians, and the more people who traveled with us, the safer I felt.

Susannah was happy. She sat on the wagon seat and watched the country pass by. She held me on her lap and talked to me about the scenery.

"Patty, look at all the wildflowers. There are so many it looks like a carpet. I've never seen so many, and so many different colors."

She was right. Wildflowers covered the prairie as far as I could see. The tall grass reached nearly to the bed of the wagon. It looked like a picture. The wagon wheels crushed some of the flowers, and Susannah talked about how good the crushed petals smelled. It made me wish my sewn-on nose worked.

"Are you going to talk to that doll the whole trip?" Almeron asked.

Susannah hugged me and smiled. "Patty's my special friend. She's the first and only doll I've ever had. I like talking to her."

Just then a rumble could be heard in the distance. Almeron looked at the sky.

"That sounds like thunder, but there aren't any clouds."

The rumble got louder. Soon I could feel the wagon begin to shake. In the distance I could see a cloud of dust rising to the sky. Suddenly the man who was guiding the wagon train came riding toward us. He was waving his hat over his head.

"Buffalo! Buffalo!" he shouted. He raced past us, and soon I saw men on horses riding toward the dust cloud. Almeron didn't have a horse to ride, so he sat on the wagon seat and watched the men ride off to hunt. The wagons had stopped, and everyone looked toward the distant herd. Now I could see a brown mass running across the prairie. The herd kept coming and coming. I began to think that it would never end.

We could hear the sound of distant pops as the men fired their guns at the running buffalo. Finally the herd disappeared over a small hill and the hunters rode after them. The wagons began to move. We rode in the direction the buffalo had taken. All of the settlers talked about the good meal they would have that evening.

We made camp, and soon campfires were cooking chunks of fresh buffalo meat. Susannah had never eaten buffalo, but she talked about how good it was. We were sharing the fire with several other people. They were talking and eating when the scout walked over to our fire.

"Sit down and have some buffalo," Almeron said.

The man sat down. "Thanks. No more buffalo for me. I've had plenty."

"That was a big herd," one of the men said.

"I've seen bigger," the scout said. "But that was sure good size."

Almeron looked at the scout. "It seems something's bothering you. What's wrong?"

The scout stared into the fire. "When I was riding after that herd, I saw arrows sticking out of some of the buffalo."

Everyone was silent, and Susannah held me close as we listened to the scout. "They were Comanche arrows. I guess that herd had been chased by Comanches before we saw it."

"What do we need to do?" Almeron asked.

"Tomorrow make sure everyone stays together. I don't know if the Comanches are still around. They might have gone home with their buffalo meat. Just keep your eyes open. I don't think they'll attack us because there are too many of us. But if you wander away, you could be in trouble."

The scout got up and walked to another campfire. Soon everyone went to bed. I lay under the blanket. I was lying face up so I could see the moon and stars. I could hear Susannah breathing as she slept next to me. It seemed so peaceful here in Texas. In the distance I heard a coyote howl. Another answered it. Soon I could hear them howling all around us.

Then I had a thought. What if they were not coyotes? What if we were surrounded by Comanches? It seemed like forever, but finally the sun rose. I was sure glad to see the light of day.

We never saw any Indians on our trip. One day we saw a herd of antelope racing in the distance. We saw many quail and other game birds. I heard the men talking about how Texas was a hunter's paradise.

"What are we going to do when we get where we're going?" Susannah asked.

"I think I'll open a blacksmith shop," Almeron said. "There's always a need for a good blacksmith. And that will give you a place to walk by every day."

Susannah hit Almeron on the arm. They laughed as we rode on. Finally we came to the edge of a small town. Almeron pulled the wagon to a stop.

"Here we are, Susannah. This is our new home."

"What's the name of our home?" Susannah asked.

Almeron took off his hat and wiped his forehead. "Gonzales. Gonzales, Texas."

Chapter Five

GONZALES WAS A GREAT PLACE TO LIVE. The people were friendly, and soon Almeron had a successful business going. Susannah was happy that I liked the new home too. One day Almeron came home early. Susannah was cooking supper, and she was surprised to se him so early.

"What's wrong, Almeron?" she asked. "Are you sick?"

"No, Susannah." He sat down at the kitchen table. "I have some news."

Susannah wiped her hands on a towel and sat down across from Almeron.

"What's the news?" she asked.

"Well, I'm going to start a new business. George Kimble and I are going to open a hat factory here."

"A hat factory? What do you know about making hats?"

"I know enough, and George knows some. We think we can do well. There's not another one around here, and everybody wears hats."

Susannah reached over and lifted me off the table. She stroked my hair as she thought about what Almeron had said.

"Well, that's right. Everyone wears a hat. I could help out. I could help with ladies' hats."

Almeron smiled. "That's right. I'm glad you think this is a good idea. I was worried you wouldn't like it."

"Texas is for people to try new things. We came here for a new life. This will be part of it. I might even make a hat for Patty."

Almeron stood up. "I need to get back to work. I'll be home a little later. Supper smells good."

He reached for some cookies that Susannah had sitting on a plate. Susannah slapped his hand.

"You go on back to work. Those cookies are for after supper."

Almeron turned to go. Susannah walked over and set me down on the counter. Almeron turned back, grabbed some cookies and ran out the door. Susannah laughed as she watched him leave. She shook her head and went back to cooking supper.

As the months went by, the hat factory began to attract more and more customers. Susannah was happy working there, and I liked to sit on the counter and watch the people try on hats.

One day Susannah left me at the store while she went to the doctor. She didn't seem sick, but I was worried about her. It seemed like a long time until she came back. She was smiling as she walked through the door. Almeron was standing behind the counter writing in a record book. He looked up as Susannah walked in.

"What did the doctor say?" he asked.

"You know you have been talking about building another room onto our house."

Almeron nodded. "As soon as I get a chance I'm going to get started. Why?"

"You better get started soon, because we're going to need the room for the baby."

I nearly fell off the counter. Almeron looked shocked, then smiled and ran around the counter and hugged Susannah.

"That's great news. I guess I better get started."

Susannah smiled. "You have a little while." She walked over to me. "What do you think, Patty? Are you ready for a little brother or sister?"

I stared out across the room. A baby. Now I was going to have to share Susannah. The baby would demand a lot of her time. She might even forget about me. I could end up in some attic, forgotten and lonely.

Susannah picked me up. "If it's a girl, you will have a new playmate. I bet she'll love you as much as I do."

Wait, I hadn't thought of that. A little girl would need a doll. I would have two friends, not just one. But what if it was a boy? Boys don't play with dolls. I could still wind up in the attic. All I could do was hope the baby was a girl.

The next few months went by quickly. I would sit and watch Susannah make clothes for the new baby. Almeron made a cradle, and sometimes Susannah would lay me in the cradle and cover me with a quilt she had made for the baby. She would rock the cradle and it felt good lying under the quilt being rocked. I could picture the little girl holding me while Susannah rocked us. I was ready for the baby to come, but then I would think that it could be a boy, and I was glad we still had some time together.

Finally the day arrived. Almeron got the doctor, and I sat on the counter while Almeron paced the floor. I'm not sure how much time went by. It seemed like days but I know it was only a few hours. Finally the doctor came out of the room. He smiled at Almeron.

"You have a fine baby daughter," he said.

Almeron ran into the room to see Susannah. I felt like jumping up and down. A daughter. A girl. Now I would have a new friend. Now I wouldn't end up in a dusty attic. Yes, life was good in Gonzales, Texas.

Chapter
Six

THE TIN SOLDIER YAWNED AND STRETCHED. He turned to the ballerina doll.

"I thought you said this was a story about a battle. All I've heard about is a girl and her doll. I think I'll go look around the attic. There's got to be something up here that's more interesting than a story about a doll."

The ballerina doll put her hand on the tin soldier's arm. "Just wait a minute. Patty's about to get to the battle part."

The tin soldier looked at the other toys. Some of them were smiling as they watched him. The rocking horse rocked slowly back and forth. "Climb on my back if you're bored," he said. "I'll give you a ride that won't bore you."

The ballerina patted the rocking horse. "Not right now." She turned to Patty. "Go on with your story, please."

Patty looked at the moonlight coming through the small window. "Where was I? Oh yes. I was talking about the new baby…"

Those days after the baby was born were some of the happiest of my life. They named her Angelina. She was a pretty little girl. Sometimes Susannah would put me in the crib with her and rock us while she sang a lullaby. As Angelina grew older she would hold me in her little hands and chew on my ear with her toothless mouth until my face was wet. Sometimes we would go outside and Susannah would spread a blanket on the ground and we would lie on it and watch the clouds drift by.

In the next few years Almeron's business continued to do well. Susannah didn't work at the hat factory much anymore. She stayed home and took care of Angelina. One day Almeron came home early, and I could tell he was worried about something. He sat at the table and looked at the coffee cup Susannah had given him. She sat next to him and put me on the table next to Angelina's chair. Angelina was trying to eat a cookie and getting crumbs all over the floor.

"What's the matter, Almeron?" she asked.

"There's some talk going around that we might be heading for trouble with the government of Mexico," he said.

"I thought the new president was well liked," Susannah said.

"Everyone thought that he was going to be a good president. But he has done things lately that have some people worried."

"What has he done?" Susannah asked.

"He's sent some troops into Texas. He is using them to collect taxes that haven't been collected in years. He says he doesn't want any more settlers coming into Texas. I think he wants to run off the ones who are here."

"I don't know why he would want to do that. We're building this country into something good. What's the president's name?"

Almeron took a drink of his coffee. "His name is Santa Anna. Stephen Austin went to talk to him and was put in jail. There are some young men who are talking about forming an independent state. That would mean going to war with Mexico."

Susanna wiped Angelina's face. "Who would want to do that?" she asked.

"One of the leaders is William Travis. More and more people are listening to him and his friends. I'm afraid there'll be trouble soon."

Susannah held Angelina in her lap. "Well, if that happens we'll just have to make the best of it."

Almeron looked into his cup. "Susannah, it's going to happen. I think it would be best if you and Angelina left Texas and went back to Tennessee until the trouble here is over."

I saw Susannah's face turn red. "Almeron Dickinson, you get that thought out of your head right now. I'm not going anywhere. My place is here with you. I'm not going to run off and leave you when there might be some trouble."

"But, Susannah. You can come back when it's safe."

"Almeron, it's not safe here now. There are Comanches roaming around. We found a rattlesnake in the flowerbed yesterday. Texas is a place for people who are strong enough to tame it. You are one of those people, and so am I. And your daughter will be too. So stop this talk about sending me away. You married me and I promised to stand by you in good times and bad. You won't get rid of me that easily."

Almeron smiled. He stood up and walked over and put his hands on Susannah's shoulders. "All right. I know when I'm licked. Whatever happens, we'll face it together."

He bent down and kissed Susannah on the top of the head. "I better get back to work. I'll see you at supper."

We watched Almeron leave. Susannah put Angelina on the floor and picked me up. She stroked my hair as we watched Angelina play with a rattle that was lying nearby. "Well, Patty. Those were brave words. I wish I felt as brave as I sounded. To tell you the truth, I'm scared. If the president sends more troops and we have a war, I'm afraid for Almeron. I know he will be in the fighting. Well, we can't worry about that now. Anyway, it's probably just talk. I bet nothing will happen."

Chapter Seven

THE NEXT FEW MONTHS WERE FILLED with stories about war coming to Texas. Stephen Austin had been locked in jail in Mexico. William Travis and his friends spoke out for independence for Texas. Several men in Gonzales formed a militia company. Almeron joined them. I could see Susannah becoming more worried every day. She would still take Angelina and me outside and put us on a blanket under a tree, but she spent most of her time watching the road into town, like she was expecting the enemy army to march in any minute.

One day we were at the dinner table. Almeron had just come home from work. He was holding Angelina. She had me by the arm and I was flopping against the chair.

Suddenly there was a knock at the door. Susannah wiped her hands with a towel as she walked to the door.

Captain Albert Martin stood in the doorway.

"Good evening, Mrs. Dickinson," he said as he removed his hat. "Is your husband here?"

Almeron got up and put Angelina down on the floor. He walked over to the door.

"I'm here, Albert. What's wrong?"

Captain Martin stepped inside the room. "There are enemy soldiers coming here from San Antonio."

"Enemy soldiers?" Almeron said. "Why would they be coming here? We haven't done anything."

Albert looked at Susannah as she picked up Angelina and held her close to her. "They want that old cannon that the government gave us about four years ago."

"That old cannon? I don't think it even works. Why would they want that?" Almeron asked.

"We think it's just the first step in taking our weapons away from us. We're having a meeting at the general store. We would like for you to come."

Almeron looked at Susannah. "Sure. I'll be right there."

Captain Martin walked out the door. Almeron walked over and picked up his hat.

"Almeron, are you sure you should go?" Susannah asked.

"Of course I should go," he answered. "We have to protect our homes and families."

"But you said the cannon probably doesn't even work. Just give it to them and there won't be any trouble."

"Susannah, remember we talked about this. We knew there was a chance that there would be trouble. Even fighting. We decided that what we have here is worth fighting for. We must make Texas a good place to raise our family. I can't sit by and let others do it for me. I must help."

He put on his hat and walked outside. Susannah sat down. She still held Angelina and Angelina still held me by the arm. I dangled in the air until Susannah took me and set me in her lap next to Angelina. Susannah rocked us back and forth and hummed a little tune. I looked at her face and saw a tear run down her cheek. We sat there for several hours. Angelina went to sleep. Susanna tucked her in her bed then sat back down and held me as she hummed the same tune. The cabin was dark with only the embers from the fireplace shedding any light in the room.

Finally we heard footsteps outside. The door opened and Almeron walked in. He came and sat in a chair next to us.

"How was the meeting?" Susannah asked.

"Fine. A rider came from San Antonio. A force of one hundred men is headed toward us. They have orders to take the cannon."

I felt Susannah tighten her hold on me. "What are you going to do?"

"We've sent some men to other towns asking them to come help us keep the cannon. We hope that soon we'll have enough men to drive off the enemy soldiers."

Susannah didn't say anything for a while. She sat and rocked.

"What if the others don't come?"

Almeron sighed. "Then we'll fight 'em with whatever we have. But I believe that soon many men will come to join us."

Almeron got up and lit a lantern. He got his rifle from above the fireplace and began to clean it. I watched him. He wasn't scared at all. He calmly cleaned his gun, then laid it across the table.

"You better get some sleep, Susannah."

"Where are you going?" she asked.

"Some of us are going to mount the cannon on some old wooden wheels. We're going to have it set up so when the enemy gets here, they'll see the cannon and it might scare them away."

"The cannon doesn't work," Susannah said.

"It might. We haven't used it in awhile. Besides, they won't know it doesn't work."

Almeron picked up his gun and walked out. Susannah and I sat in the chair and looked into the fire. I don't know how long we sat there; I just knew that the night seemed awfully long and awfully dark.

Chapter Eight

SUNLIGHT BEGAN TO PEEK THROUGH THE WINDOW. Susannah had fallen asleep in the chair. Angelina rolled over in her bed and made little noises. I sat in Susannah's lap and watched the room begin to lighten as the sun rose. Suddenly there was a knocking on the door. Susannah woke with a start and looked around the room. She stretched and put me on the table. She stood up and walked to the door. A neighbor woman was standing there.

"Hello, Elizabeth. What are you doing out so early?" Susannah asked.

"Hurry, Susannah. Get your daughter and come with me."

"Where are we going? What's happening?" Susannah asked.

"The enemy army is here. Our men have set up a

blockade to stop them, but we only have eighteen men. The enemy has many more. The women are going to that little group of trees down by the river. It's safer there."

"Where's Almeron?"

"He's with the other men. Hurry. We don't have much time. The enemy could start shooting any minute."

Susannah ran over and lifted Angelina out of her bed. She quickly put some clothes on her and hurried to the door. I lay on the table. Was she going to leave me to the enemy? I wanted to call out to her to come back for me, but I just lay there.

Susannah joined Elizabeth at the door. They walked outside. Susannah reached back to shut the door. She looked up and saw me lying on the table.

"Just a minute, Elizabeth. I have to get Patty." She walked back inside.

"Who?" Elizabeth asked. She saw me and said, "Forget that old doll. We need to be going."

"I can't leave Patty. She's been with me too long. I would rather stay than leave her." Susannah ran to the table and picked me up. She hurried outside and shut the door to the cabin.

The streets of Gonzales were filled with people hurrying around. Most were headed for the wooded spot next to the river. I saw a group of men standing around the old cannon. They were looking across the river at a group of soldiers who were marching steadily toward them. I saw a flag waving above the cannon. It was a white flag, and there was a picture of a cannon with the words "Come and Take It" painted on the flag.

We stopped running when we reached the woods. Other women were there with their children. We settled in and watched the soldiers as they stopped on the far side of the river across from our men. The leader of the soldiers rode forward and shouted to our men. I could not hear what he said or what our men said back to him. Soon the officer turned around, and his men marched back a short way and made camp. I could see our men talking, and then a man walked away from the group and headed toward the trees. As he got close enough, one of the women called to him.

"What's going on, Andrew?"

The man stopped and looked at the women and children.

"They've come for the cannon. That officer wanted to talk to the mayor, but we told him that he wasn't here. He's going to wait for him to come back."

"Where are you going?" Susannah asked.

"I'm going to get some more men from the towns around here. My horse is in back of these trees. I hope to get more men here before the enemy attacks. Now, ladies, I really have to go."

The man walked to his horse. He mounted and rode away. We looked back toward our men. They were still standing around the cannon, watching the enemy make camp. Susannah held Angelina by the hand and held me in her other arm.

Elizabeth turned to the other women.

"Well, it seems that there won't be any fighting for awhile. I don't know about your men, but my husband gets awfully grouchy if he doesn't get his breakfast. I'm going to get him something."

She walked out of the woods toward her house. Susannah and the other women followed her. Before long Susannah had made some breakfast for Almeron and we took it to him. Other wives were there, and soon it looked like a picnic was taking place. Small boys climbed on the cannon, and dogs chased each other as the families ate. We sat next to Almeron and watched the enemy camp. They were cooking and setting up tents. They did not appear in any hurry to attack us.

"What's going to happen, Almeron?" Susannah asked.

Almeron wiped his mouth on his sleeve and looked across the river at the enemy.

"They want our cannon. We don't want to give it to them. I don't think that the officer wants to fight us for it, but he has his orders. I just hope other men get here before he decides he has to attack us to get the cannon."

"Do you think other men will come?"

Almeron smiled and nodded. "They'll come. Texas is their home too. They love it as much as we do. We won't be pushed around in our own homes. I bet before tomorrow we have plenty of men."

Susannah held me close to her as she looked across the river at the enemy troops. I could feel her heart beating as she held me. I knew that if I had a heart, mine would be beating just as fast. She turned and looked the other way. I knew she was looking for more men coming to help us. The countryside was empty as far as the eye could see. She turned around and looked at the enemy camp again. She reached over and took Almeron's hand. He was holding Angelina. So here we were. A family sitting together, looking across the river at an army of enemy soldiers waiting to attack us.

Chapter Nine

MEN BEGAN TO ARRIVE IN GONZALES. The enemy had remained in their camp and had not attacked. The women and children spent some time in the woods and some time in their homes. We had just returned to our house when word came that an enemy attack was expected and we should return to the woods. Susannah carried Angelina, who held me by an arm as we hurried toward the woods. I could see the men standing in a group looking toward the enemy camp. There were over one hundred men here now.

When we reached the woods, Susannah turned around. I knew she was looking for Almeron. He must have been standing in the middle of the group, because we could not see him. As we stood looking at the men, Elizabeth walked over to us.

"Are you all right, Susannah?" she asked.

Susannah nodded. "I'm fine. I just wish they would go away and leave us alone," she said, pointing toward the enemy camp. "I don't know why those men have to fight over that silly cannon. It's not worth getting killed over."

Elizabeth smiled. "I talked to John about this last night. It seems that the men don't believe they're just fighting for the cannon. They believe they're fighting for Texas. The president of Mexico, Santa Anna, wants to drive us out of Texas. Our men think Texas is worth fighting for."

Susannah looked around. "Texas is a beautiful place. There's an awful lot to like about it."

Elizabeth nodded. "Yes, Texas is beautiful, but she demands a lot from the people who want to live here. You can start a new life in Texas, but it won't come easy."

The sound of firing caused the women to look toward the enemy camp. The Texans had crossed the river and were walking toward the enemy camp. We could see the smoke from the rifles and hear the distant pop of the muskets. The enemy returned the fire, and the Texans took cover. The firing stopped as suddenly as it had begun. We waited the rest of the day for the fighting to start again, but there was only silence.

When night came, Susannah wrapped a blanket around us. We lay on the ground listening to the sounds of the night. Small animals scurried through the brush. An owl hooted from a nearby tree. In the distance a coyote howled and another answered. Sometime during the night a thick fog covered the area. Early the next morning the guns began to fire again. We couldn't see what was happening. We could only see the flash of the muskets in the foggy air.

Suddenly a roar shattered the air as the cannon was fired. Angelina started to cry. Susannah held her close and whispered to her. The other women and children huddled together and listened to the sounds of the battle. Sometimes we could hear the sound of a man yelling, but we could not understand the words.

Finally the fog lifted and we could see the men across the river firing at the enemy. Once a stray musket ball whizzed overhead and smacked into a tree. After a long time the firing stopped. We tried to see what was happening, but we were afraid to stick our heads too far out of the trees. Suddenly we saw a man riding his horse along the riverbank, headed toward us. As he got near, one of the women called out,"What's happening?"

The man took off his hat and waved it toward the enemy camp. "They're leaving. They're headed back to San Antonio."

The women came running out of the trees and looked toward the enemy camp. In the distance we could see the last of the enemy soldiers disappearing from view. Susannah looked toward the Texan army. I could tell she was trying to find Almeron.

"Was anyone hurt?" she asked.

The man shook his head. "I don't know. The rifle balls were flying pretty thick, but I didn't see anyone get shot."

We could see the men walking back toward the town. We hurried down to the river crossing to meet them. Susannah held Angelina by the hand and held me in her other arm. She searched the faces of the returning men but did not see Almeron. I could tell she was beginning to worry, and a tear ran down her face. Other women were hugging their husbands and walking toward their homes. Suddenly someone put his hand on Susannah's shoulder. She turned and saw Almeron smiling at her.

"Almeron, I'm so glad to see you." She hugged his neck.

"I'm glad to see you too. I was down river a little ways and crossed there. Are you all right?"

Susannah smiled and nodded. "I am now. I was so worried that something had happened to you."

"Well, it was pretty hot there for awhile, but our muskets and cannon were too much for them. They should be well on the way back to San Antonio now. You know, fighting sure makes a person hungry. Let's go on home and get something to eat."

Almeron picked up Angelina, and Susannah held me as we walked back toward our house. It was good to know that the fighting was over and that we were all safe.

Chapter Ten

"IS THAT ALL THERE WAS TO YOUR BATTLE?" the toy soldier asked. "That wasn't much of a fight. I'm wasting my time here. It'll be light soon, and I want to check out this attic. Not listen to more doll stories."

"My word, you are so impatient," the ballerina said. "Just listen. There is a lot of fighting coming up. Go on, Patty. I think this is so interesting."

Patty looked at the tin soldier and smiled. "You remind me of all the young men back then. They were so eager to get into a fight. Even Almeron. Oh well, there was much to learn. Now where was I?..."

The days following the fight at Gonzales were busy. Men rushed about, forming groups and trying to decide what to do next. Some of the men who had come to help went home, but others stayed. Then one day Almeron rushed into the house. He grabbed his gun and began to pack some clothes.

"Almeron, what are you doing?" Susannah asked.

"We just got word that Stephen Austin is leading an army to San Antonio. We are going to drive the enemy out of San Antonio and out of Texas."

Susannah grabbed the back of a chair. "No. Why do you want to go looking for a fight? It was one thing to fight when your home was threatened, but you shouldn't go off to another place and leave your family alone."

Almeron walked over to Susannah and put his arms around her.

"What we did here was only the beginning. We showed 'em we would fight for our independence. Now we have to make 'em leave Texas. If we let them stay, they'll get stronger and it'll be harder to make them go. There are already men in San Antonio. More will come, like they did here. I must go help them, like others came to help us."

"What about us? What about Angelina and me?"

"You'll be fine here. Some of the men are staying. Mr. King said he would check on you. If I thought you were in danger, I wouldn't leave you. I'm going to make sure the danger leaves and doesn't come back here again."

Susannah walked around the chair and sat down. She picked me up from the table and held me in her lap. She watched Angelina play in front of the fireplace. Almeron walked over and finished packing his clothes.

"How long will you be gone?" she asked.

Almeron shook his head. "I don't know. Not long, I think. When the enemy sees we are serious about defending our land, I think they'll leave. Then we can make a fine home here for all of us."

He finished packing and walked over to Angelina. He picked her up and gave her a kiss. Susannah stood up. Almeron hugged her, then picked up his things and walked to the door.

"Don't worry," he said. "I'll be back before you know it."

He shut the door and walked away. The house suddenly felt very empty.

The days went by and Susannah waited for word from Almeron. Sometimes a messenger from San Antonio would ride through town. People would gather around him asking for news of the battle and if he knew whether their loved ones were all right. More volunteers passed through Gonzales on their way to San Antonio to join the army. Some of them were rough-looking men who scared the women and children as they marched through town. We were all glad when these men left.

One day Susannah was sweeping the floor. I was lying on the table and Angelina was napping in her cradle. Suddenly there was a knock on the door. Susannah opened the door, and two of the rough-looking men were standing there.

"Howdy, ma'am," one of them said. "We are on our way to join the army in San Antonio, and we was wondering if you would give us something to eat?"

"I'm sorry, I don't have anything for you right now." Susannah tried to shut the door.

One of the men pushed against the door and knocked Susannah back into the room. She grabbed a chair to keep from falling to the floor. The men came inside the house. They looked around.

"This is a nice house. I bet you have some things here

we could use," one of them said.

The men began to walk around the house. They took some things and put them in their pockets.

"Put my things back and get out of my house," Susannah yelled at them.

The noise woke Angelina, and she started to cry. One of the men picked me up.

"This is the ugliest doll I ever saw. I think I'll throw it in the fire and make this room look better."

His friend laughed as he carried me toward the fireplace. I was scared. He raised his arm to throw me into the fire when Susannah hit him in the back with her broom. He dropped me to the floor and turned to Susannah.

"Why did you do that? That's no way to treat a guest in your house."

He began walking toward Susannah. She started swinging her broom at him and yelling as loudly as she could. I lay on the floor and watched as his friend tried to sneak up behind Susannah. She turned and hit him in the head with the broom. The man backed up, covering his head. When her back was turned the first man grabbed Susannah and held on as she struggled to get free. The other man grabbed the broom from her.

"Now," he said. "I guess we need to teach you some manners."

"I don't think so." A voice from the door made everyone turn around. Mr. King and a few others stood in the doorway, pointing guns at the two men who held Susannah.

"Let the lady go," Mr. King said. "Then be on your way. There's plenty of fighting to be done in San Antonio."

The men let Susannah go. They walked out the door.

Mr. King and the others watched them until they were out of sight. Susannah picked up Angelina and held her until she stopped crying. She reached down and picked me up. Mr. King walked back into the house.

"Are you all right, Susannah?" he asked.

Susannah nodded her head. "Yes. Thank you."

She walked over and grabbed her old suitcase from under the bed.

"What are you doing?" Mr. King asked.

"I'm going to pack my things, then we're going to San Antonio."

"You can't go there," Mr. King said. "There's fighting there. It's not safe."

"I don't think it will be any worse than here. Besides, that's where Almeron is. If there's trouble, I need to be with my husband."

Chapter Eleven

"SUSANNAH. WHAT ARE YOU DOING HERE?" Almeron asked as we walked into the room where he was staying.

"Two men broke into our house and looted it. I don't know what we would have done if Mr. King hadn't been there," Susannah told him.

"I'm glad you're all fine," Almeron said as he hugged Susannah.

Susannah walked to the door and looked outside. Men were busy clearing the streets and taking some cannons toward an old mission across the river.

"What's going on here, Almeron?" Susannah asked.

"We had quite a battle here. We finally got the enemy commander, General Cos, to agree to take his troops and leave Texas. We're trying to get this place cleaned up and to make that old mission stronger in case the enemy comes back."

Susannah turned back into the room. "Do you think they will come back here?"

Almeron walked over and picked up Angelina. "There are stories that Santa Anna is heading this way with a large army. General Cos was his brother-in-law. He won't like it that Cos agreed to leave Texas and never return. I imagine that he will come to take San Antonio back, but we think he won't come before spring. A large army with all of its animals will need food, and there's not much food on the prairie in the wintertime."

Susannah walked back over to the door. "Why are the men taking the cannons into that old mission?"

"We're going to make that old mission into a fort. It's going to be so strong that the enemy won't be able to take it."

Susannah stroked my hair as she turned to Almeron. "That old mission doesn't look like it could be made into a fort. The walls are falling down, and the chapel doesn't even have a roof on it. Besides, it looks like it will take more men than I see around here to defend it."

Almeron walked over and put an arm around Susannah. "By the time Santa Anna gets here, we'll have the mission built into a strong fort. And more men will come to join us. Don't you remember how the men came to Gonzales? We'll be fine. Now I think you need to go somewhere safe until the fighting is over. I can send you back to Tennessee or at least to East Texas, where you'll be safe and you can get back to the United States if you need to."

Susannah shook her head. "Almeron, I already told you. I'm not going to leave you. I'm your wife. I'm going to be with you in the bad times as well as the good. Now quit trying to get rid of me. It seems the first thing we need to do is find a house for all of us to live in. Oh, what did you say the name of that old mission was?"

Almeron walked over to the door and looked outside. "They call it the Alamo," he said.

The next month went by fast. We found a home in the Ramon Musquiz house. Susannah took in boarders and did laundry for the men to earn some extra money. More men came to San Antonio. Jim Bowie rode into town one day with several other men. We were sitting in front of the house watching the activity in the town when he rode in. He was a big man, and I saw the famous knife hanging at his side. He went into the house where Colonel Neill, the commander of the troops, was staying. A little while later, Almeron came home. We were in the house cooking when he rushed in.

"Susannah, Jim Bowie is here," he said.

"Yes, we saw the men ride in. I thought it was Bowie when I saw his knife."

Almeron sat in a chair. "He has orders from Sam Houston to blow up the Alamo and leave San Antonio."

Susannah looked up. "When are we leaving?"

Almeron smiled. "We're not. Colonel Neill convinced him that San Antonio is too important. We're going to stay and Bowie is staying with us. With men like Jim Bowie, we can beat Santa Anna for sure."

Susannah walked over and picked me up. I could feel her heart beating as she held me close. She looked at Angelina sleeping in her bed. She didn't say anything, but I saw a tear on her cheek as she stirred the stew she was cooking.

More men came to San Antonio as the weeks passed. Others left. William Barrett Travis rode into town with some men. He was a young man, but you could tell he was ready for a fight. One day Colonel Neill left the Alamo, and he left Travis in charge of the troops. When the men found out, they were not happy. They wanted Jim Bowie to lead them. The men held an election and Bowie won. It was decided that Bowie would lead the volunteers and Travis would command the regulars. Both men would sign all letters from the army.

Susannah kept busy running the boarding house. One day there was a knock on the door. When Susannah opened it, she saw a tall man wearing buckskins standing there. The man took off his coonskin cap when he saw Susannah.

"Hello, ma'am," he said. "I heard you had room for a boarder."

"Yes we do," Susannah said.

"Well, I would like to rent a room from you. My name is David Crockett from Tennessee."

Chapter Twelve

"WAIT A MINUTE," THE TOY SOLDIER SAID. "You mean you knew Davy Crockett? And Jim Bowie? And William Travis? Are you saying you were at the battle of the Alamo? That's one of the most famous battles of all time."

The ballerina doll smiled and put her hand on the toy soldier's arm. "Let Patty go on. It'll be dawn soon and we'll have to go back into hiding."

Patty smiled at the toy soldier. "I knew all those men. And I was at the Alamo. It was a long time ago…"

Susannah smiled at the tall man standing in the doorway. "Congressman Crockett. Please come into the house. Of course I have a room for you."

The tall man walked inside. He looked around the room. He smiled at Angelina. "Please, don't call me Congressman. The voters didn't want me, and I am just as glad. After traveling through Texas, I've decided that I would rather be in my present station than to be elected a member of Congress for life."

He walked over and picked up Angelina. "Who's this pretty little girl?"

Susannah walked over and picked me off the floor where Angelina had dropped me. "My daughter, Angelina."

Davy held her up toward the ceiling. "Well, she is as pretty as her mother. I kissed my share of babies when I ran for office, but I don't think I ever saw one as pretty as her."

I could see Susannah smile as she held me. "Why, thank you, Congressman… I mean, Mr. Crockett."

"Please call me David. Or Davy, if you believe the stories."

"Well, Davy, come with me and I'll show you to your room. Do you have any luggage?"

"Not much. I travel light."

Davy followed us to his room. He still held Angelina, who was playing with the tail on his coonskin cap. I could tell that it was going to be fun having Davy Crockett in the house.

The next several weeks went by fast. The men worked to strengthen the Alamo. Almeron attended several meetings with Travis and Bowie. They were making plans for the arrival of Santa Anna's army. Scouts sent out by Juan Seguin reported that the army was on its way, but Travis didn't believe it. He thought that they would wait until spring. He didn't believe that Santa Anna would move a large army across the barren plains in the wintertime.

Sometimes in the evening we would sit outside the

house. Susannah would hold me while Davy bounced Angelina on his knee. Men would gather to hear his stories. They howled with laughter when he described the San Antonio River as looking like a snake with the bellyache because of all the turns and twists. Sitting there listening to his stories and hearing Susannah and the men laugh, it was hard to imagine that an enemy army might be marching toward us.

One day Almeron came home and told us that there was going to be a big party that night. It was in honor of George Washington's birthday. There would be lots of food and dancing. Susannah was excited and hummed all day as she did her chores around the house.

That evening we all walked to the plaza. People were already there. A small band was playing, and the sound of guitars and fiddles filled the air. The smell of food cooking made me wish that I could eat. We found a table and watched the people dancing in the plaza. Men would stop by to talk with Almeron and some of the ladies stopped to hold Angelina and talk to Susannah. Almeron got some food and they ate while they listened to Davy Crockett play his fiddle. A Scotsman named John McGregor had some bagpipes and he played a few songs on them. The bagpipes sounded strange in contrast to the guitars and fiddles.

As the evening wore on I saw Juan Seguin lead a man over to the table where Travis was sitting. They talked, and then I saw a man go and get Jim Bowie and Davy Crockett. They stopped by our table and told Almeron that Travis wanted him to come over to his table. I saw the worried look in Susannah's eyes as she watched him walk over to the small circle of men. We couldn't hear what they were saying, but it appeared that Travis and Bowie were arguing and Crockett was trying to keep peace among them. At last the meeting broke up. Almeron walked back to the table and sat down. There was a worried look on his face.

"What was the meeting about?" Susannah asked.

Almeron sighed. "Juan Seguin's scout brought word that Santa Anna's army is very near. Travis doesn't believe it and Bowie does. They got into quite an argument. Davy Crockett tried to keep the peace, but it's not good to have the commanders of the army fighting with each other if the enemy is near."

"What are they going to do?"

"Travis is putting a sentry in the old bell tower to watch for any sign that the enemy might be near. He'll send out some patrols tomorrow to see what they can find." Almeron stood up and took Angelina, who had fallen asleep. "Let's go home. Tomorrow might be a busy day."

Chapter Thirteen

A RINGING CHURCH BELL SHATTERED THE STILLNESS of the morning. Almeron came running from the bedroom, pulling on his trousers as he ran. Davy Crockett was close behind him. They left the door open as they ran outside. I could see people running down the street toward the sound of the bell. Susannah came out holding Angelina. She walked to the door and looked toward the bell tower.

Soon the bell stopped ringing. For several moments it was very quiet. Then I saw people walking back. Some were laughing and shaking their heads. Finally Almeron walked through the door.

"What happened?" Susannah asked.

"The sentry thought he saw enemy soldiers on the prairie. He rang the bell as a warning, but when Travis and Bowie got up to the tower they couldn't see anything. Most people thought the sentry had too much fun at the party last night and saw things that weren't there."

"What are they going to do now?" she asked.

Almeron took the cup of coffee that Susannah gave him. "Travis is sending a couple of men out to check the area. If they see anything they're to ride back fast. If the sentry sees them coming back at anything faster than a walk, he's to ring the bell and we'll all move into the Alamo."

"I guess I better pack some things," Susannah said.

Almeron stood up. "Oh, I don't think there's anything out there. Besides, we can't take very much into the Alamo. I'm going down to the stables and check on my horse. I'll be back soon."

The next several minutes seemed to crawl by. The door was still open, and I could see people walking down the street. Every now and then they would look toward the bell tower. Susannah worked around the house while Angelina played with me. I was beginning to believe the people who said the sentry had seen something that was not there, when I heard the bell ring again. Susannah ran to the door.

"What's happening?" she called to a man running by.

"The enemy army's here. Everyone needs to go to the Alamo as soon as possible."

Susannah ran over and picked up Angelina. She was holding me by the arm and I swung around as Susannah ran to the door. She ran out into the street calling for Almeron. People were running up and down the street. Some pushed carts loaded with their possessions. Others carried bags of clothes. Some just had their muskets as they ran toward the Alamo. Susannah looked all around as she yelled Almeron's name.

Suddenly he came riding up. He pulled his horse to a stop right by us.

"Almeron, what are we going to do?" Susannah asked.

"Don't ask questions. Give me the baby and climb up behind me," he said.

Susannah handed Angelina to him and climbed up behind him. Angelina was still holding me by an arm. I was afraid she was going to drop me. As Susannah put her arms around Almeron, she took me from Angelina and held me in both of her hands.

We rode down the street heading for the bridge that led to the Alamo. Ahead of us I could see people rushing through the Alamo's open gates. When we got to the bridge, it was crowded with people. There was no way for us to cross there without waiting. Almeron guided his horse down the river until he came to a place where we could cross. The water splashed on me as the horse ran through the shallow water. When we got to the other side of the river, Almeron headed for the open gate. We rode into the Alamo courtyard, and Almeron stopped his horse in front of the old chapel. Susannah slid down from the horse and took Angelina from Almeron.

"Go inside the old chapel and find a room," he said. "I'll put up the horse, then I need to take my place on the walls. I'll be back as soon as I can."

We walked into the old chapel. There was no roof, and debris covered the floor. An earthen ramp rose to the roof-line. Several cannons sat on a platform at the top of the ramp. Susannah walked to the back of the chapel and found a small room. We walked in, and as our eyes adjusted to the darkness, we saw that other people were already there. I knew most of the people from seeing them around San Antonio. Ana Esparza was there with her four children. Her husband, Gregorio, was somewhere in the Alamo.

Juana Alsbury and her sister Gertrudis Navarro, sisters-in-law to Jim Bowie, were there. A young girl named Trinidad Saucedo and an old woman named Petra Gonzales were also in the room.

We could hear the men as they took their positions on the wall. Susannah took Angelina and me and walked out into the courtyard. We could see a group of men standing on the wall looking toward the town. Almeron was standing by a cannon that pointed toward San Antonio. We walked over and climbed up next to Davy Crockett.

I could see a large red flag waving from the bell tower of the San Fernando church. One of the men said that meant there would be no mercy in the coming fight. The enemy army was still marching into the town square. I had never seen so many soldiers.

Finally one of the enemy rode toward the Alamo. He stopped his horse in front of the wall where we stood watching. He pulled a paper out of his coat and read the message to us. Santa Anna asked if we wanted to surrender. If we did not, he said he would kill every man in the Alamo. When he had finished, he looked up at Colonel Travis.

"What is your answer?" he asked.

Travis looked around him at the men. They were watching him. He looked at the enemy army still marching into San Antonio. He looked at the red flag blowing in the breeze. Finally he turned to Almeron.

"Captain Dickinson. Fire the cannon," he said.

Chapter Fourteen

EVERYONE STARED AT TRAVIS. Almeron held the burning match above the cannon. He looked around at the other men. Everyone knew that if the cannon was fired there would be no turning back. Susannah held her breath as she looked at Almeron. The messenger stared up at the men, waiting for an answer.

"Captain Dickinson," Travis said again. "I said, fire the cannon."

Almeron took a deep breath and touched the match to the cannon. The cannon erupted in a great roar. Smoke poured out of the barrel, and for a minute I couldn't see anything. Some people wiped their eyes when the smoke drifted into them. Susannah and several others jumped when the cannon roared. When the smoke cleared I could see the cannonball bouncing down the street. It rolled into the wall of a building and stopped. The messenger turned his horse and rode back to the enemy lines.

Colonel Travis turned to the men. "All of you go to your positions now." He looked at Susannah and some of the other women who were standing there. "Ladies, I suggest that you go to your rooms. It will be safer there. I imagine that Santa Anna will have an answer to our reply soon."

The men started to walk away. Almeron took Angelina, and Susannah and I followed him down the ramp. Behind us I could hear Bowie and Travis arguing about the cannon shot.

"Almeron, what will happen now?" Susannah asked as we walked across the courtyard.

"I imagine Santa Anna will attack soon. He'll be mad about the cannon shot."

"Why did Travis order that?" she asked. "He had to know it would make Santa Anna mad. Now there's no hope of making peace."

"There was never any hope of making peace. Santa Anna wants war. He wants to punish the Texans. He'd like to drive us out of Texas. Travis knows that. We all know that. When we came in here we knew there would be a fight. I just hope more men come soon. I'm just sorry that you and Angelina are here. It's going to be dangerous."

Susannah reached out and touched his arm. "I've told you, my place is with you. There's no place I would rather be right now than with you."

Just then I heard a roar. It sounded like thunder, but there were no clouds in the sky. I saw men running. Almeron grabbed Susannah's arm and started to run toward the chapel.

"Hurry, Susannah. That's a cannon firing. Santa Anna is answering our shot. We have to get inside the chapel."

We ran across the courtyard and through the door of the chapel just as the cannonball exploded outside. I heard broken pieces of the cannonball strike the chapel walls.

"Susannah, get in the room. I have to get to my cannon," Almeron said.

We watched him run up the ramp, then we hurried inside the small room where the other women and children were already waiting. We found an empty spot and sat down. Susannah rocked Angelina and held me as we listened to the cannonballs land inside the Alamo.

Some of the children were crying and a few of the women were praying as we listened to the cannonballs. Every now and then the Texans would fire their own cannons and the sound would echo off the walls of our small room. When Almeron fired his cannon, the flash would light up our room and the smoke would drift down and fill the nostrils of the women and children. One cannonball struck the wall of the chapel and made our room shake. I thought that the walls would fall down at any minute.

Suddenly, as quickly as it had begun the cannon fire stopped. I could hear our men cheering. Susannah and the others sat in the dark room and wondered what had happened. I could tell that Susannah was worried about Almeron. Mrs. Esparza tried to comfort her children.

Juana Alsbury got up and walked to the door. She slowly stuck her head outside the door and looked around. The interior of the chapel was filled with smoke. She took a few steps outside of the chapel, then called back into the room.

"I can't see much. I see some men on the gun platform,

but I can't tell who they are."

Susannah got up and walked out of the room with Angelina and me. She stared up at the gun platform through the smoke.

"Almeron, are you all right?" she called.

"I'm fine, Susannah," Almeron's voice drifted to us out of the smoke. "We're all fine."

I could feel Susannah relax with relief as she heard Almeron's voice. Mrs. Esparza called to us from inside the room.

"Is my husband, Gregorio, all right?"

"Almeron said everyone is fine," Susannah answered.

Suddenly Juana and Susannah became aware of a man running toward them in the gloom of the chapel. He stopped in front of the women when he recognized Juana.

"Mrs. Alsbury," he gasped. "Come with me. Jim Bowie is very sick. He needs you."

Juana called to Gertrudis and the two women followed the man out of the chapel. Susannah walked back into the room and sat down. I could tell she was very tired. All of the women seemed tired, and the battle was just beginning.

Chapter Fifteen

THE NEXT DAY SUSANNAH TOOK ANGELINA AND ME and walked outside the chapel. The sunlight was bright after we had been in the dark room for so many hours. The fresh air felt good although there was beginning to be coolness to it. The enemy cannons were firing, but they were not doing much damage to the walls. Men were working to make the walls stronger. There were some fires burning in the courtyard, and some men were roasting meat over the fires.

Colonel Travis was talking to a man on horseback. He handed the rider some papers, and the man rode to the front gate. The gate opened and the man rode out. The gate was quickly shut as the messenger galloped away.

"How are you, Susannah?"

The voice startled us. Susannah turned and saw Davy

Crockett standing there.

"Oh, Davy. I'm doing all right. Where was that rider going?"

Davy looked toward the gate. "Travis sent him as a messenger to try and get some more men to come here. If they come soon, there won't be any problem for them to get in here. The whole enemy army isn't here yet. There are still some gaps to get through."

Susannah looked around the Alamo. A cannonball thudded against the wall and some rock chips sailed through the air.

"You better get back inside," Davy said. "It's not real safe out here right now."

Susannah took a deep breath of the fresh air. "It feels so good out here. It's so dark and small in that room. I like it better out here."

Davy nodded. "I know what you mean. I would rather march out and fight them in the open. I hate to be hemmed in."

Susannah saw Juana walk into a small room carrying a bowl of food.

"What's wrong with Jim Bowie?" she asked.

Davy shook his head. "The doctor says he has consumption. He was coughing a lot. Yesterday he just fell down and couldn't get up. I'm afraid he's out of this fight. Travis is the only commander now."

Susannah felt tears come to her eyes. "Davy, do you think more men will come?"

Davy smiled. "Sure they will. Why, as soon as they get Travis's message I bet more men will be here than you can shake a stick at. We'll send Santa Anna and his army high-tailing it back the way they came."

"I hope you're right," Susannah said. "We will miss Jim Bowie. He was a real fighter."

"Yes. We need men like Bowie. But we have other good men. All these men are good men, and they want to fight for Texas."

Almeron came walking out of the chapel. He walked over to Susannah and Davy.

"Here you are," he said. "Mrs. Esparza said you came outside. How are you Davy?"

"I'm fine, Almeron. Well, I'll leave you nice folks for now. I need to see how Bowie is doing."

Susannah and Almeron watched him walk away. Almeron took Angelina and gave her a hug. "You shouldn't be out here, Susannah. It's too dangerous."

"Oh, Almeron, it feels so good out here. It's so small and stuffy in that room. The cannonballs are not even coming close. Let's go get something to eat."

Almeron smiled. "I guess it won't hurt to come out here sometimes. I'm hungry. That meat sure smells good."

We walked over to a fire, and a man cut some meat for Susannah and Almeron. There were some corn tortillas, and Angelina chewed on one of those. They ate their meal in silence. Men came to the fire for some food and then went back to their posts. When they had finished eating, Almeron turned to Susannah.

"You better get back inside now. The weather's getting colder. There are some blankets in one of these rooms. I'll bring you some."

"Bring some for Mrs. Esparza too. Her children will need them."

We walked back into the chapel. It took a while for our eyes to adjust to the dim interior. We walked around the debris on the floor and headed toward the room. Someone had built a small fire outside the room. The smoke drifted slowly out of the open roof. We walked into the room and saw Mrs. Esparza holding her daughter. The little girl was sleeping. Her three brothers were playing in a corner of the room. No one else was in the room.

Susannah smiled at Mrs. Esparza. She sat down and leaned against the wall. We could hear the wind start to whistle. The temperature in the room began to drop. Susannah pulled her shawl tighter around her shoulders and hugged Angelina to her to keep the little girl warm. The small fire outside the room didn't provide much warmth. Almeron walked in the door carrying an armload of blankets. He gave some to Mrs. Esparza and handed a couple to Susannah.

"It's getting cold out there," he said. "A norther just blew in. These blankets should help. I have to get back to my cannon. I'll see you later."

We watched him walk out of the room. Susannah took a blanket and wrapped it around us. We sat in silence in the dark room, huddled together against the cold, and listened to the cannons fire at the Alamo. It seemed that if the cannonballs didn't kill us, we would freeze to death.

Chapter Sixteen

IT GOT COLDER WHEN THE SUN WENT DOWN. We stayed huddled under the blanket. Angelina was asleep, but Susannah stared through the doorway at the dying embers of the fire outside. Mrs. Esparza covered her sleeping children with a blanket and leaned against the wall. She closed her eyes but was unable to go to sleep.

The enemy cannons continued to fire, and the thudding of the cannonballs against the walls of the Alamo filled the women with dread.

"I wish that the cannons would stop. If only for a little while," Mrs. Esparza said.

"So do I. The constant noise is hard on my nerves." Susannah looked at the sleeping children. "Mrs. Esparza, why did you bring your children to this place? You had a home in San Antonio. You could have stayed there or gone out into the country with some friends."

Mrs. Esparza opened her eyes and smiled. "I came here for the same reason that you did. My husband is here. My place is with him. Oh, he tried to get me to stay or go with friends, but I told him I would not let him face this danger alone. I told him if he comes with me, I will go."

Susannah nodded her head. "I understand. I told Almeron the same thing. He told me that he thought Texas was worth fighting for and that he was willing to fight to give his family a good home. A home that was free, where we could be safe."

"Yes, Gregorio said the same. He could have stayed out of the war, but he joined Juan Seguin's company and followed him here." Mrs. Esparza raised her head and looked at the ceiling. "He has a brother in Santa Anna's army. One of my sons, Francisco, is named for him. I remember the last time they were together. They argued over Texas. Francisco said Gregorio should support Santa Anna and fight the Texans, but Gregorio said no. He said Santa Anna was a dictator and he would not support a man like that. He wanted his children to grow up in a free country. Now they are fighting against each other."

"It seems our husbands think alike," Susannah said. "I guess every man here thinks that way. I just hope others come soon. I know we can't hold off Santa Anna's army with just the men we have here."

Susannah stood up and stretched. Mrs. Esparza looked up at her.

"Why don't you go outside for a little while? I'll watch the children."

Susannah stooped and picked me up.

"Thank you. I won't be long."

"That's a nice doll you have."

"I've had her a long time. I guess she's my best friend. I'll be back soon."

Susannah wrapped a blanket around us and we walked outside. The wind was blowing, and Susannah stayed next to the walls to block the cold air. Next to the chapel was a log fence. Davy Crockett and his men guarded the fence. Some of them sat around a small fire warming their hands. We walked over to the fire, and Davy stood up when he saw us coming.

"Hello, Susannah. Enjoying your evening stroll?"

"I just came out to get some fresh air."

Davy laughed. "Well, there's certainly a lot of that out here. Help yourself to all you want."

As we sat by the fire, the cannons began to slow down their firing. Soon there was silence. The men grabbed their rifles and went to the log fence. They stared into the darkness to see if the enemy was attacking. Suddenly the sound of music filled the air. The enemy band was playing as loudly as it could. The men stayed on watch, fearing an attack.

"Why are they playing that music, Davy?" Susannah asked.

Davy listened for a few minutes, then sat back down by the fire. "I think it's just another way of keeping us awake. Santa Anna wants to wear us out so that when he does attack, we'll be too tired to fight."

Susannah looked at the men standing at the fence. Their eyes strained to see into the darkness. Their faces already looked tired.

"Davy, don't you think we should leave now while we can? We're going to be trapped here soon. When the rest of the enemy army arrives, there won't be any escape."

"Well, Susannah, that might make sense. But Travis, Bowie and the others have decided that this is the place to make a stand. We need to stop Santa Anna here before he gets to the settlements. They believe others will come to fight with us and we can beat Santa Anna here."

"What do you think, Davy?" Susannah asked.

Davy took a deep breath and stared into the fire. "I think it's a lot harder to kill a bear out in the open than one that's trapped in a cave. Right now I feel like a bear trapped in a cave."

Chapter Seventeen

IT WAS STILL COLD, BUT THE WIND had stopped blowing. The enemy cannon continued to fire, and the band played loudly all night. It was hard for everyone to sleep. The women and children were as tired as the men. We stayed in our small room most of the time. We listened to the cannonballs thud against the walls of the Alamo and wondered when the walls would cave in.

One afternoon Susannah took Angelina and me and we walked up the ramp to the cannon platform, where Almeron leaned against the cannon watching the enemy camp. Gregorio Esparza was visiting his wife and family. The other men were huddled around the small fire in the chapel. Almeron smiled as he saw us walk up to him.

"Susannah, you really shouldn't be up here. It's very dangerous."

Just then a puff of smoke rose from an enemy cannon, and we heard the roar as a cannonball arched toward the Alamo. The shell fell short of the wall, throwing up a spray of dirt and rocks that bounced harmlessly off the old mission's walls.

"If that's the best they can do, I think we're safe enough," Susannah said.

Almeron took Angelina and held her as he looked back at the enemy lines.

"They move closer every day. I expect they'll attack soon."

Susannah held me with one hand and put her other on Almeron's shoulder.

"Davy Crockett wants to go out and fight them in the open. He feels trapped in here," she said.

Almeron laughed. "I expect he does. But if we hold on a little longer, men will come to join us. Travis has sent some more messengers out, and I look for reinforcements any day."

We looked at the enemy camp. We could see where the cannons were shooting from. Behind them were rows of tents where the enemy soldiers slept. Many soldiers drilled in the distance. I could see the sun shine off their bayonets as they marched. The scene made me afraid. There were so many enemy and so few Texans.

"Why don't you come down and sit by the fire for a while?" Susannah asked as she pulled her shawl tighter around her shoulders. "It's cold up here."

"I'm all right. The men need to warm up some, and Gregorio needs to see his family. I'll be down later."

Susannah turned and looked around the Alamo. Some men blew on their hands to keep them warm as they stared at the enemy lines. Others sat around small fires at the bottom of the wall. Some of the men wrapped up in blankets and tried to sleep.

"How long can these men hold on, Almeron?" she asked.

Almeron looked at the men. He smiled and put his arm around Susannah.

"As long as they have to. These men are dedicated to Texas. They'll do what they have to so that Texas can be free."

Down in the courtyard Colonel Travis was talking to a man on horseback. He handed the man some paper. He put the paper in his saddlebags and walked his horse toward the gate. Travis waved to some men on the north wall. Soon firing broke out on the wall. Texans were yelling and shooting. While the enemy fired back at the Texans, the gate opened and the rider rode out. He raced his horse down the road and rode between two enemy cannon positions before the enemy soldiers could stop him. Soon he was out of sight.

"See, Susannah?" Almeron pointed in the direction the rider had ridden. "There goes another messenger. I bet he's going to Goliad and Colonel Fannin. He's got the most men of anyone around here. When he gets here, we'll be fine."

Susannah tried to smile, but I could see the worry in her eyes. "Surely Colonel Fannin knows about us by now. He should be on his way already."

"I bet he is," Almeron said. "This messenger will just make him come faster."

We stood next to Almeron for a while. No one spoke. It just felt good to be together as a family, even if there were thousands of enemy soldiers not far away. One of the men sitting around the fire laughed, and we looked down into the dark interior of the chapel. We could see the glow of the fire and the shadows of the men who sat around it.

Almeron shook his head. "These are very special men. They could be feeling sorry for themselves, but their spirits are high. You'd think they didn't have a care in the world. I'm proud to be serving here with them."

Susannah leaned against Almeron. "I'm proud to be your wife. When this war is over, I know we'll have a good life in Texas."

Once again we stood in silence. Even though the enemy cannons still fired, I felt that surely everything would turn out all right. Yes, before long more men would come, this war would be over, and we would have our happy home again.

As we stood there together, I heard a man shout.

"The enemy are attacking!"

Chapter Eighteen

When we heard the shout, we turned and saw many enemy soldiers running toward the Alamo from a group of small shacks. Men along the wall that was being attacked began to fire at the running soldiers.

"Susannah, get back to your room," Almeron called.

We started to go down the ramp, but the men who had been sitting by the fire were running toward the cannon. We stood aside as they ran past us. Gregorio Esparza was the last to get to the platform. When he passed us, we hurried down the ramp. We heard Almeron yelling at the men to turn the cannon toward the attacking enemy as we reached the bottom of the ramp.

Just as we entered the small room with the other women and children, the cannon fired. The flash lit up our room and the blast echoed off the walls. A woman screamed and some of the children began to cry as the smoke from the cannon drifted into the room and filled our nostrils.

Susannah sank to the floor and leaned against the wall as the cannon fired again. We could hear rifles firing and men yelling. It seemed like the firing went on forever. Susannah held Angelina and me close to her as we listened to the fighting.

Suddenly the firing stopped.

"They're running away," someone yelled.

Men began to cheer. The women sat in the dark room and waited to see what would happen. We could hear Almeron yelling to turn the cannon back around. It seemed like hours until we saw Almeron come into the room.

"Susannah, where are you?" he called.

"Over here, Almeron." Susannah stood up as he walked toward us.

"Is Gregorio all right?" Mrs. Esparza asked as he went by her.

Almeron looked down at her and smiled. "He's fine. The enemy has pulled back. The fighting's over for now."

Almeron hugged us to him. "Are you all right?" he asked.

"We're fine. I was so worried about you. The fighting was so loud."

Almeron smiled. "I guess it was loud in this little room. But the walls are thick enough that this is the safest place for you. I don't think the enemy will attack again very soon. If you want to we can go outside and find something to eat." We walked toward the door when we heard someone call Almeron's name.

"I'm in here," he called.

We walked out into the chapel and saw Colonel Travis standing at the foot of the ramp. We walked over to him.

Travis took off his hat when he saw Susannah.

"Mrs. Dickinson, I hope you and your daughter are all right," he said.

"We're fine, Colonel. Just a little scared."

"I can understand that," Travis said. He turned to Almeron. "I want you to turn your cannon back around toward those little shacks," he said. "Davy Crockett's going to take some men and burn them down. They let the enemy get too close to us. I want you to cover them in case there are still enemy soldiers in those shacks."

Almeron nodded. "When are they going?"

"As soon as it gets dark. Hopefully the enemy has pulled out of them, but Jim Bowie thinks there might still be some enemy in them."

Almeron called up to the men on the platform, and they began to turn the cannon once more. Travis turned and walked outside. Almeron watched as the cannon was turned. Then he looked at Susannah. "Come on. Let's go find something to eat."

It was beginning to get dark as we walked outside. We found a fire where meat was being cooked. Almeron and Susannah got some food and sat by the fire to eat. While they were eating, Davy Crockett walked up. He was carrying a torch in his hand.

"Sit down and have something to eat, Davy," Almeron said.

"Thanks, but I'm going to be doing some running real soon, and I don't want anything to slow me down. I'll eat when I get back."

"Well, Davy," Susannah said. "It looks like you're going to get your wish."

"What do you mean?" he asked.

"You said you wanted to go fight them in the open, and now you're going to go outside and fight them."

Davy smiled. "I guess I should be more careful about what I ask for. Well, it's nearly time. I better be going. I'll see you in a little while."

We watched Davy walk away. Almeron stood up. "I guess I better get back too. You better go back to your room in case there's any more fighting."

We walked back into the chapel with Almeron. We watched him walk up the ramp. Susannah started to go into the room, but then turned and walked out into the courtyard again. Davy Crockett and a group of men were gathered around Colonel Travis. Some of the men carried torches. The men walked over to a small gate and stopped. Travis turned toward the north wall. He took off his hat and waved it at the men on the wall. The men began to fire at the enemy. Soon the enemy started firing back at the north wall. Travis shook Davy's hand. The small gate opened and the group of men rushed through it.

Susannah walked over to the log fence, and we watched the men run toward the wooden shacks. Soon they reached the shacks and began to throw their torches into them. As flames began to burst from the shacks, enemy soldiers ran from them. Davy and his men began shooting at the enemy. More enemy soldiers were running toward the fight. Davy and his men would not be able to get back across the open ground into the Alamo.

Travis yelled to the men who were watching the fight, and soon they were firing at the enemy. Almeron gave the signal, and his cannon fired into the advancing enemy. This slowed them down, and Davy and his men jumped up and ran toward the open gate. The enemy fired at them, and bullets kicked up puffs of dirt around their running feet.

The cannon fired again, and soon the running Texans rushed through the gate and fell to the ground. They lay there trying to catch their breath. The other Texans cheered as they watched the shacks burn. Colonel Travis walked over to Davy.

"You and your men did a good job, Davy."

Davy sat up. He looked over at Susannah and smiled. "I never thought I'd say this, but I'm sure glad to be back inside these walls."

Chapter Nineteen

THE NEXT DAY WE WALKED OUT OF THE CHAPEL to get some fresh air. We saw a group of men standing around a man on a horse. We walked closer to the men and heard Colonel Travis talking to him.

"Juan, be sure and tell the reinforcements to bring plenty of ammunition and food with them. We don't have any to spare."

Juan Seguin looked down at the men standing around him. "Colonel Travis, I told you before. I shouldn't be the one leaving. I brought other men into the Alamo with me. It's not right for me to leave them here. You need to send someone else."

Travis shook his head. "I told you, Juan. You're the best choice to go. I don't know if any of my messengers made it through the enemy lines. We desperately need men and supplies. You speak Spanish and you know the country around here. Juan, if anyone can get through the lines and bring more men back, you can. You can be of more help to your men by bringing reinforcements than by staying here. Just go get some more men, then come back. Your men will understand."

Davy Crockett reached up and patted the horse's neck. "He's right, Juan. We're all counting on you. Be sure and hurry back. I want to take you up on your claim that you're a better shot than me."

Juan and Davy shook hands. Juan looked toward his men, who were standing on the wall watching. He waved to them. He looked back at the group of men standing by his horse.

"All right. Thank Jim Bowie again for loaning me his horse. I'll be back, my friends. I promise."

Juan turned his horse and walked to the gate. The gate slowly opened and Juan rode out. We could hear his horse's hooves pounding on the hard ground. We listened until the sound faded away. The group broke up and the men walked toward their posts. Davy walked over to Susannah.

"How are you doing?" he asked.

"I'm doing all right. I hope Juan can bring more men soon."

"So do I," Davy said. He looked around the Alamo. "There he is."

"Who?" Susannah asked.

"John McGregor. I heard he thinks he's a pretty good bagpipe player. Well, I know I'm a good fiddle player. So I'm going to challenge him to a contest. Tonight we'll show the enemy what real music is." Davy walked toward John McGregor. He turned and called to us, "Be sure and come to the contest tonight. It should be fun."

We walked back into the chapel. Almeron was walking down the ramp as we walked toward our room.

"Hello, Susannah. Been outside?"

"We watched Juan Seguin leave to get reinforcements. I hope he can bring some back soon."

Almeron looked out over the open roof of the chapel. "If anyone can bring them back, Juan can. I feel better knowing he's gone to get more men."

Susannah leaned against Almeron. "Davy Crockett and John McGregor are going to have a contest tonight to see who can play the loudest on their fiddle and bagpipes. Come with me to see it."

Almeron looked up at the men standing by the cannon. "I think I can get away for awhile. It should be fun. Well, I better go let some of the others take a break. I'll see you after while."

It was dark when Almeron and Susannah walked out of the chapel and toward a group of people that were gathering around a fire. Mrs. Esparza was watching Angelina while she slept in the room. The enemy cannons still fired but not as often. The enemy band had not started to play yet. Some men carried Jim Bowie next to the fire. He lay on his bed looking very tired. He was very thin and coughed as he talked to the men. Travis stood on the outside of the crowd.

Davy Crockett and John MacGregor walked to the middle of the circle of people.

"Well, I'm glad to see so many of you could be here tonight," Davy said. The crowd laughed. "John and I are going to have a contest to see which one can play the loudest. Jim Bowie has agreed to judge the contest. So I guess we'll get right to it."

Davy and John MacGregor begin playing their instruments. Slowly at first, but then gaining speed and getting louder as the crowd began to cheer. The music became so loud that it was hard to hear the enemy cannons when they fired. As they continued to play, a tune began to develop. Soon people were clapping their hands and stomping their feet in time with the music. A couple of men began to dance. Others joined them. Almeron and Susannah began to dance. They whirled around. Susannah held me by the arm, and the people and the fire rushed by my eyes as we danced around and around.

Davy and MacGregor began to play another tune. Someone cut in, and Almeron stood aside as the man danced with Susannah. Others cut in, and soon there was a line of men waiting for a chance to dance with Susannah. We whirled and stomped and danced for what seemed like hours. The men clapped and cheered like they didn't have a care in the world. Soon the music stopped and people gasped for air and clapped for more music.

Davy held up his fiddle. "I think it's time for Jim Bowie to tell us who won the contest."

All the men looked at Bowie as he lay on his bed. He coughed then tried to sit up. When he spoke his voice was weak, and the men leaned forward to hear what he had to say.

"I must say that was probably the worst bunch of noise I've ever heard. In fact, it was so bad I can't decide who was worse. I guess you're going to have to do it again another time and maybe then I can tell who won."

Davy looked around the circle of men. "I guess I can go another time. How about you, John?"

"I reckon I can go again too."

The men all cheered at the news of another contest. Colonel Travis walked into the middle of the circle.

"Men, this was fun, but now it's time to return to your posts."

We watched the men walk away. Some of them carried Jim Bowie back to his room. Almeron took Susannah's arm and we walked toward the chapel.

"That was the most fun I've had in a long time," Susannah said.

"Yes, it was fun. When this battle's over we're going to go to a real party and dance all night."

As we walked into the chapel, the enemy cannon fired and the band began to play.

Chapter Twenty

THE NEXT FEW DAYS DRAGGED BY. Susannah spent some time standing at the cannon position looking out over the prairie for any sign of reinforcements. The enemy cannons moved closer to the Alamo each day. Each day the pounding of the cannonballs weakened the walls of the old mission. The men worked hard to strengthen the walls, but they could not keep up with the damage done by the constant pounding.

Sometimes we walked around the courtyard. The men were friendly and spoke to Susannah and patted Angelina on the head. Almeron rarely left his cannon position. Like all the men, his face was covered with stubble of beard and his eyes were sunken and dark from lack of sleep. The men still laughed and joked, but you could tell the constant strain was wearing them down.

I was very dirty by now. Susannah took me everywhere she went, and the smoke and dust kicked up by the cannons soon covered me. Susannah was tired too. She napped when she could, usually when Angelina was sleeping, but it never seemed to be enough sleep.

Travis sent out more messengers. We waited every day for word from those already sent out. Soon Susannah began to believe that none of the messengers had made it through the enemy lines. Not even Juan Seguin.

One evening just after dark we were sitting in our room. Suddenly we heard a sentry on the wall shout, "Who's there?"

There was silence for a few moments, then someone fired a rifle.

"Don't shoot. We're Texans," shouted a voice from outside the walls. "Open the gate."

Susannah jumped up and carried me with her as she ran out of the chapel. By now Colonel Travis was running toward the wall.

"What's going on?" he yelled to the sentry.

"There's a group of men outside the walls. They claim to be Texans and want to come in," the sentry answered.

Travis climbed the wall and called down to the men outside the wall.

"Where are you from?"

"Colonel Travis. Is that you? I'm John Smith. I brought some reinforcements."

Travis turned to the men standing by the gate. "Open the gates. Hurry."

The gates were opened and we watched as a group of men rode into the Alamo. The gates shut when the last one rode in. The men stopped their horses in the courtyard and began to dismount. Travis ran up to the leader of the group and shook his hand.

"John. It's good to see you. How many men did you bring?"

John Smith took off his hat. He looked at the group of defenders watching him.

"I brought thirty-two men from Gonzales. That's just about every able-bodied man in the town."

When Travis heard the number of men who had come, you could see the disappointment cross his face. He tried to hide the disappointment as he smiled at John Smith.

"That's good, John. Have you heard anything from Colonel Fannin?"

Smith looked around the Alamo. He scratched his head and put his hat back on.

"We thought he'd be here. We expected to meet him on the way here, but when we didn't find him, we thought he must have come on ahead of us. You mean to say he's not here?"

Travis shook his head. "No. Maybe he's on his way. Well, we're sure glad to see you men." Almeron was standing next to Susannah. Travis looked at him. "Captain Dickinson. Show these men where to put up their horses and get them some food. I imagine they're hungry. I'll talk to you later, John. I need to finish a letter I was writing."

Travis walked toward his room. Davy Crockett walked up to John Smith and shook his hand. "Good to see you, John." He turned to the defenders who were standing nearby watching. "Let's give a cheer to the brave men from Gonzales. We're happy to have them join us."

The men cheered and waved their hats in the air. Almeron took the men and showed them where to stable their horses. Davy talked to John Smith as we stood nearby.

"How hard was it to get through the enemy lines?"

Smith shook his head. "Not really all that hard. They have men all around the Alamo, but there are some gaps in their lines."

Davy rubbed his chin. "So others can make it through to us too."

Smith nodded. "That's right. Fannin can march his army in here with no problem."

"Well then," Davy laughed and slapped John Smith on the back. "We'll just have to wait for him to come. By the way, John, John McGregor and I have a little bet going about who can play the loudest. I'd like to get the opinion of you and your men."

Susannah watched as Davy and John Smith walked away. She hugged me tight and said, "See, Patty? It's going to be all right after all. These men came tonight. I bet tomorrow more men will come, and soon we'll have enough to beat Santa Anna and send him back home. Come on. Let's go get some rest."

We walked back to our room happy that at last more men were starting to come.

Chapter Twenty-One

THE ENEMY CANNONS NEVER STOPPED FIRING. Luckily no one had been badly hurt by the shells. We spent more time in our room because the cannons had moved closer and more shells fell into the courtyard.

Everyone was tired. Between the cannons and the band, it was almost impossible to get any sleep. The men took naps when they could. They would wrap themselves in blankets and lean against the wall and sleep for a few moments. It was still cold, but the wind wasn't blowing as hard as before. We still had food, but it was beginning to run out.

Whenever he had a chance, Almeron would come into our room and sit next to Susannah. He would hold Angelina and she would hold me, and we would enjoy being a family as long as we could. I always hated to see Almeron walk out the door and head back to his cannon. We didn't know if we would ever see him again when he left us.

Still, the morale of the men was good. Davy Crockett and John McGregor still had their contests. They always raised the spirits of the tired Texans.

The men spent a lot of time looking for signs that reinforcements were coming. Every time we would see a group of men approaching, it would turn out to be more of the enemy army arriving in San Antonio. Once when we climbed the ramp to stand with Almeron, we saw enemy soldiers working behind their lines.

"What are they doing, Almeron?" Susannah asked.

Almeron had a telescope that he looked through. He looked for quite a while, then put the telescope down and shook his head.

"They're building ladders. I guess they'll make an attack before too long."

Susannah took the telescope and looked at the enemy soldiers. Her hands shook as she watched them. When she put the telescope down, her face was pale.

"There's so many of them. When do you think they'll attack?"

Almeron gazed at the enemy lines. "I don't know. They have enough men to attack any time. There were more that came today. Travis still thinks Fannin or someone else will come. I'm beginning to think nobody is coming. I'm afraid we'll have to fight them with what we have here."

As we stood watching the enemy, we heard a man shout, "There's a rider coming."

We looked in the direction the man was pointing and saw a man riding as fast as he could toward the Alamo. There was a white handkerchief tied around his hat. A group of enemy horsemen were chasing him. Travis ran to the top of the wall and watched the rider.

"That's James Bonham," Travis said. "I told him to tie a white handkerchief around his hat when he came back so we would know it was him."

The rider was getting nearer to the Alamo. The enemy cavalry was starting to close the gap between them and Bonham. Travis pointed to the rider and yelled to Davy Crockett. "Shoot at the enemy. Give Bonham some cover."

Davy and his men began to fire at the enemy cavalry. The enemy stopped and rode away, and Bonham raced his horse through the open gate. As he pulled his sweating horse to a stop, the men cheered. Travis rushed up to him as he dismounted. The men shook hands and Travis took Bonham into his office.

Everyone watched the door to Travis's office as they waited for the news that Bonham had brought. Men talked about the chance that he was bringing news that reinforcements were on the way. Some men laughed for the first time in days as they thought about the large number of men they were sure was marching toward the Alamo.

It was late in the day when Travis stepped out of his room and called to one of his officers. He spoke quietly to the man and then went back inside. The officer walked around to the men who were watching and told them to gather in the courtyard in thirty minutes. Colonel Travis wanted to talk to them.

"What's he going to say?" one of the men called.

"I guess you'll have to be here in thirty minutes to find out," the officer said.

Almeron turned to Susannah. "You better get back to the room. It's safer there."

Susannah shook her head. "I'm going to be there when

Travis talks to you. I want to know what's going on too."

At last the time for Travis to speak to the men arrived. The men stood in a line in the courtyard. Some of the men had carried Jim Bowie outside. He lay on his bed and talked to some of the men. Finally the door to Travis's office opened, and Travis and Bonham walked out. Travis stopped in front of the men while Bonham took his place in the line. Travis stood looking at the men for several minutes. Finally he cleared his throat and began to speak.

"Men, James Bonham brings us bad news. It seems that Colonel Fannin is not coming to join us, and as far as Bonham knows, no other troops are on the way."

When she heard these words, Susannah gripped me tighter. From where we stood I could see the faces of the men. Some looked sad, while others stared straight ahead.

"As you know," Travis continued, "I've sent out many messengers asking for more troops. When we came into the Alamo, I truly believed that more men would come to fight with us. Now it seems we must fight the enemy alone. There are some choices for you. If you choose, you are free to leave. You have done all anyone could ask of you. No one can attach any blame to you should you decide to go."

The men stared at Travis. I wondered what they were thinking as Travis continued to speak.

"I have made my choice. I will stay and fight for Texas. I believe that Texas is worth fighting for. I hope that by fighting Santa Anna here, even if he wins, it will be worse for him than a defeat."

Travis walked to the end of the line of men. He took his sword and drew a line in the sand. He walked back to the center of the men.

"Those of you who are willing to stay with me and fight for Texas, cross the line."

For a few moments no one moved. Then one young man walked across the line and stood next to Travis. More men followed him. Davy Crockett, James Bonham, Gregorio Esparza, and then Almeron. I heard Susannah take a deep breath as she watched Almeron cross the line and stand with the others. Soon only two men remained across from Travis. One was Jim Bowie, who tried to get up from his bed but was too weak. The other was a man named Louis Moses Rose. No one spoke until Bowie called out to the men standing by Travis.

"I would like to join you boys, but it seems I can't get up. I would appreciate it if some of you would give me a hand across the line."

Four men ran to Bowie, lifted his bed, and carried him across the line as the other men cheered. Now only one man stood on the other side of the line.

"You don't seem willing to die with us, Rose," Bowie said.

Rose shook his head. "No. I won't if I can help it."

"You might as well come over with us," Davy Crockett said. "You can't escape."

Rose looked at the men standing across the line. He turned and looked at the wall. "I have done worse things than to climb that wall," he said.

Rose walked over and picked up his bundle of clothes. He climbed to the top of the wall. He looked down at the men who were watching him and waved. He jumped to the other side of the wall and disappeared in the darkness.

"Thank you," Travis said. "Now we need to get back to our posts. I think the enemy will attack soon."

We watched the men walk away. Almeron walked over to Susannah. He put his arm around her, and they walked into the chapel. I was proud of him and all the men who had crossed the line. They were willing to fight so that Texas could live, but I was afraid that in doing that, they would all die.

Chapter Twenty-Two

THE NIGHT SEEMED DARKER THAN USUAL as we sat in our small room. Susannah hummed softly as she rocked Angelina. Mrs. Esparza spoke softly to her children as they huddled against her. The other women in the room sat quietly, staring at the blank walls. I lay in Susannah's lap, thinking how peaceful it was sitting in the almost silent room.

Then it hit me. It was silent. The enemy cannons had stopped firing. It was strange not hearing the constant roar of the cannons and the explosion of the shells. Susannah noticed it also. She sat listening and then whispered to Mrs. Esparza.

"The cannons have stopped firing. What do you think is happening?"

Mrs. Esparza looked out of the door. She listened for a few minutes, then turned to Susannah.

"I don't know. I don't hear our guns firing either."

Susannah stood up. "I'm going outside to find out what's happening."

She carried Angelina and me, and we walked out of the room. Up on the gun platform we could see the men looking toward the enemy camp. Almeron was not with them. Susannah called up to the men. "Where's Almeron?"

Gregorio Esparza walked to the edge of the gun platform.

"Colonel Travis called him to his office. They're planning for the enemy attack."

Susannah turned and carried us outside the chapel. We stayed close to the wall, trying to stay as warm as we could. We looked around the Alamo. A few men were standing on the walls watching the enemy lines. Most of the others were rolled up in blankets next to fires trying to get some sleep since the enemy cannons weren't firing. It was a dark night with little light from the moon or stars. It felt good to be outside in the cool, fresh air. Susannah took several deep breaths, and I wished my nose worked so I could smell the clean air.

Several men walked out of Travis's room. Almeron and Davy Crockett walked toward us. When they got to us, Almeron took Angelina and held her.

"What have you been talking about?" Susannah asked.

Davy Crockett took off his coonskin hat and rubbed his head.

"We're trying to decide why the enemy quit shooting at us. The best guess is they're going to attack soon and they want us sleeping. Travis has sent some men outside the walls to give us an early warning if there is an attack. I just hope those men can stay awake."

Almeron looked at Susannah. "How are you doing?"

She smiled back at him. "I'm doing fine. I keep hoping that Sam Houston or someone will ride through those gates with enough men to send Santa Anna running back to Mexico."

Davy laughed. "It's good you haven't given up hope. Maybe Santa Anna will hold off long enough for some others to get here. Well, I better go see how Jim Bowie's doing. I told him I'd bring him a couple of pistols. I'll see you later."

We watched Davy walk away. We stood silently, leaning against the old chapel walls. Finally Almeron handed Angelina back to Susannah.

"I better get back to my cannon. The men will be wondering where I'm at."

"Almeron, when I saw you cross that line, I was proud of you. Part of me wanted you to stay on the other side with Mr. Rose. Maybe we could get through the enemy lines and get away and have our life together somewhere else. But Texas is where we need to make our home. And I'm glad that you're going to be part of the army that makes Texas free."

Almeron hugged us. "When this war's over we'll make us a good home on good land. We'll look back and think this was worth it then. I better be going."

We watched Almeron walk into the chapel. I could tell Susannah didn't want to go back to the room yet. We watched Travis walk around the courtyard talking to the men who were sitting around the small fires. He walked toward us. He stopped in front of us and took off his hat.

"How are you this evening, Mrs. Dickinson?" he asked.

"I'm doing fine, Colonel Travis. How are you?"

"Considering everything, I guess I'm all right. It's nice

to have a little quiet time." Travis looked at Angelina. "You have a nice family, Mrs. Dickinson. Your husband is a fine soldier and a good man. You also have a lovely daughter. I have a son. His name is Charles. I left him with some friends when I came to the Alamo. When this war is over, if I survive, I plan to make him a fine home. If I don't, then he will have the memory that his father was a man who died defending his country."

"I'm sure we'll all make it through this war, Colonel," Susannah said. "Then you can bring your son to visit us and we'll talk about the time we had here."

Travis smiled. "I better go. I need to check on a few things. You should get some sleep while the enemy's not shooting at us."

Travis started to walk away, then stopped and walked back to us. He took a ring from his finger. It was made of hammered gold and had a black cats-eye stone set in it. He reached into his pocket and pulled out a piece of string. He ran the string through the ring and tied a knot in it. He reached over and put the string around Angelina's neck.

"I'd like to give this ring to your daughter. Just a little keepsake from me."

Susannah looked at the ring. "Thank you, Colonel. I know she'll always treasure it."

"Well, good night."

We watched Travis walk toward his room. Susannah turned and went back inside the chapel.

It was quiet in the small room. Everyone was sleeping. Susannah sat down and rocked Angelina to sleep. Soon she was sleeping also.

I sat there in the darkness for several hours, listening to the soft breathing of the sleeping people. Suddenly I heard the sound of cheering coming from outside the Alamo. Then I heard the sound of thousands of feet running on the hard ground. A rocket exploded above the chapel and the light cast strange shadows inside our room. Some of the Texans began to fire, and I heard one of them shout.

"Colonel Travis, the enemy's attacking."

Chapter Twenty-Three

IN A MATTER OF MINUTES OUR QUIET NIGHT was changed into a world of noise. The roar of the cannons and the explosions of the shells covered the sound of running feet. I could hear men yelling, but I could not understand what they were saying. The rifles fired rapidly. The sound reminded me of a string of fireworks I had heard one time at a Fourth of July celebration.

Everyone in our room was awake. We could tell that this was the main enemy attack. The children were crying and the women were praying out loud. Susannah held Angelina close to her and tried to get her to stop crying. Mrs. Esparza gathered her children to her and did her best to comfort them.

Sometimes a cannonball would thud against the walls of the chapel, and the old walls would shake and a fine dust would fall on us. The firing was continuous now. We could not have heard each other if we had tried to speak. I had never been so scared. Almeron's cannon fired, and as the flash lit up our little room, I could see the fear on the faces of the women and children as they huddled together.

It seemed like forever, but it couldn't have been longer than thirty minutes when I heard a man yell, "There they go!"

I heard men cheering. Then there was silence. It seemed strange for everything to be so quiet.

Susannah looked around at the other women.

"Did we win?" she asked.

Just then a man yelled, "Here they come again!"

Once more I heard the sound of running feet drumming on the hard ground. Then the cannons began to fire again, followed closely by the rifles. Once more I heard men yelling, and the flash of the cannon fire lit up the room. I slid from Susannah's lap and lay on the floor. From where I lay I could see the door. I saw a man run into the room next to ours, where the powder was stored. Soon he ran back carrying a small barrel of powder.

"Turn the cannon over there," I heard Almeron call. Shortly after that I heard a blast as the cannon was fired.

"Reload," Almeron called out. "Hurry."

Several more shots were fired from the cannon. The flashes cast strange shadows on our walls. One of the women stood up and tried to run out of the room, but someone grabbed her and held her as she sobbed.

"They're running again," I heard someone call. The men were cheering again.

"Gregorio," I heard Almeron say. "Go down and get some more powder."

I heard the sound of feet running down the ramp. Soon I saw Gregorio's head look through the doorway.

"Are you all right?" he asked.

Mrs. Esparza looked at him. "We're all right. We're just scared. What's happening?"

"The enemy has pulled back, but I think they'll charge again. We don't have much powder left. Almeron thinks that if we can make them run away one more time, they won't be back."

Mrs. Esparza patted one of her children. "I hope he's right," she said.

"I have to go. We need more powder. Just stay in here and you'll be all right."

Gregorio's face disappeared, and I heard him next door rolling a powder keg around. I listened as he rolled the keg up the ramp. The women sat in the room not saying a word. Once again the silence seemed strange after the noise of the battle.

"Maybe they won't attack again," someone said.

"I hope not," Susannah answered.

Just then a cannon fired. "Here they come!" a man called.

Immediately the sound of running feet again filled the air. Once more the shouts of the men and the roar of the cannons echoed off our walls.

"Keep firing," Almeron shouted. The cannon roared and we could hear the sound of the men hurrying to reload it. Suddenly I heard someone yell.

"They're over the north wall!"

The women drew in their breaths when they heard this. Now the enemy was inside the Alamo. The sound of muskets firing increased as the defenders turned to meet the large numbers of enemy soldiers climbing over the wall.

Suddenly I saw Almeron come running through the door. He stood in the doorway looking in the darkness for Susannah. Finally he saw us and hurried to us.

"Sue. The enemy are inside our walls!" He grabbed Susannah and hugged her and Angelina. He finally let them go and stood up. "If they spare you, save my child."

Susannah reached for him as Almeron hurried out the door.

"How is Gregorio?" Mrs. Esparza called to him. But Almeron was already out the door. We heard his footsteps as he ran up the ramp to his cannon.

The noise was worse than ever. The rifles and cannons never stopped firing. The smoke from these weapons was filling the nostrils and burning the eyes of the women as they listened to the sounds of the fight. We could hear the voices of the Texans as they yelled to each other. Now there were different voices speaking a different language. The enemy soldiers were getting closer to our room.

Suddenly, I could hear Davy Crockett as he yelled at the enemy. His strong voice rang out above all the other noise. I could hear him for several minutes, then the firing became louder and his voice was drowned out. As we sat in our room, we could hear the sound of the firing dying out. We were afraid of what that meant. We knew that the Texans were being killed.

We heard some men talking outside our room. "You cover me. I'll throw this torch into the powder room and we'll blow up a bunch of them," one of them said.

We heard the sound of a man running toward the room next to us. I lay there waiting to be blown up by the exploding powder. All at once there was the sound of several rifles firing. We heard a sound like someone falling, and then it was quiet in the chapel.

By now the firing had stopped except for an occasional shot. The women looked at each other and wondered what would happen to them when the enemy found them. We could hear men walking around in the chapel. The voices of enemy soldiers drifted into our room.

Suddenly an enemy officer stood in the doorway. He looked around the room then called out in English. "Is there a Mrs. Dickinson in here?"

Chapter Twenty-Four

NO ONE SAID A WORD AS WE SAT in our small room looking at the enemy officer who stood in the doorway. A couple of the women looked at Susannah. I felt her hold me tight as she sat there. The only sound in the room was the breathing of the women and the sobs of the children.

The officer looked around the room. Finally he called out again. "Is there a Mrs. Dickinson here? Speak up if you value your life."

Susannah got slowly to her feet. She held Angelina and me as she looked at the enemy officer.

"I'm Mrs. Dickinson," she said softly. I knew that she thought she would be taken out and killed.

Two enemy soldiers rushed into the room and grabbed Susannah. She nearly dropped Angelina and me but managed to hold on to us.

"Let her go," the officer said to the soldiers. "Please come with me, Mrs. Dickinson."

Susannah walked out of the room. As we entered the chapel we could see signs of the battle everywhere. Susannah looked up to the top of the ramp. Bodies of the defenders were lying around the cannon. One was draped across the barrel of the gun. Susannah gasped as she thought she recognized Almeron, but the soldiers hurried her out of the chapel.

The scene in the courtyard was like a bad dream. Smoke from several small fires mixed with the smoke of the cannons and rifles, and the sun, which was just rising, gave an eerie glow to the area. Enemy soldiers were walking around checking the bodies of the Texans. Every now and then there would be a rifle shot.

As we walked through the courtyard I saw Davy Crockett lying on the ground. His coonskin cap lay by his side. Some of the enemy soldiers stopped and looked at us as we walked past. We headed toward the gate, and one of the soldiers took Angelina from Susannah and carried her. Susannah clung tightly to me as we walked out of the Alamo.

It seemed to take forever to walk from the Alamo to a house in town. The officer told us to wait outside, then walked into the house, followed by the man carrying Angelina. Susannah tried to follow Angelina, but the guards in front of the door would not let her pass.

Susannah cried as we waited. The shocking events of the past several hours had left her tired and afraid. Sometimes she would look toward the Alamo, and I knew she was thinking about Almeron and all our friends who lay within the old mission.

Finally the door opened and the officer motioned for

us to enter. We walked slowly into the house, and we were shocked by what we saw. A man in a fancy uniform with gold braid and medals on his chest sat behind a desk holding Angelina on his knee. When I saw him I could tell right away that I did not like him. Susannah walked up to the desk and stopped. She looked at Angelina, who was bouncing on the knee of the man behind the desk.

No one said anything as we stood there. The man behind the desk did not look up at us as he played with Angelina. At last he turned and looked at Susannah.

One of his officers stepped forward and said, "Your Excellency, this is Mrs. Susannah Dickinson. Her husband was one of the Alamo defenders. Mrs. Dickinson, this is General Santa Anna, the president of Mexico."

When I heard his name, I knew I didn't like the man sitting behind the desk. If I could have, I would have attacked him as he sat there smiling at us. Susannah said nothing. She just looked at Angelina, who was playing with one of the medals on Santa Anna's chest.

Santa Anna said something to the officer in Spanish. The officer turned to Susannah.

"The president says he is happy to meet you. He is sorry that your husband chose to be a rebel and fight against him."

I saw Susannah's face turn red. She took several deep breaths and finally spoke.

"My husband was a brave man. All of the men in the Alamo were brave men. They believed in freedom and they believed in Texas. They knew they would die if they stayed in the Alamo, but they were willing to die for Texas and the ones they loved. I'm proud of my husband and all of them. They gave Texas a chance to live."

The officer told Santa Anna what Susannah had said. I saw his eyes narrow and his face turn red. He controlled his anger and said something to the officer.

"The president says you are very brave. He respects you, but he has no respect for the rebels who turn on their government. They got what they deserved. All rebels who choose to fight against him can expect the same thing."

Susannah stood there and did not reply. Santa Anna smiled at her and said something to the officer.

"The president says he has some good news for you."

Santa Anna said something else to the officer. The officer looked shocked. He didn't say anything. He looked from Santa Anna to Susannah. Santa Anna said something else to the officer.

"What did he say?" Susannah asked.

The officer looked uncomfortable, but finally said, "The president says you have a nice daughter. He likes her very much. To show his respect for you and his fondness for her, he will adopt her, take her to Mexico City, and raise her there."

Chapter Twenty-Five

SUSANNAH STOOD IN SILENCE BEFORE SANTA ANNA. She did not know what to say to him. Finally she began to shake her head.

"I could never let my daughter go with the man who killed her father," she said.

Santa Anna looked at Susannah as he waited for the soldier to tell him what she had said. The soldier looked uncomfortable. He did not want to tell Santa Anna what had been said. He looked at Susannah.

"Mrs. Dickinson, I wish you would change your mind. The president will take good care of your daughter. She will have whatever she wants. I think she will be very happy. He might even let you come with her."

Susannah shook her head. "I will never send my daughter with him. She could never be happy with someone like him. I want her to remember her father. He was a brave man. He fought for what he believed in. He died so she could live in a free country. All the men in the Alamo felt the same way. I'll always remember them and tell the world about them. I'll tell about Santa Anna too. And I'll never forget what he has done."

Santa Anna was growing impatient. He asked the soldier what Susannah had said. The soldier told him. I saw Santa Anna narrow his eyes as he looked at Susannah. I thought he would order his men to kill her. One of his generals spoke to him. The general pointed to Susannah and then to Angelina. Santa Anna listened to him then nodded. The general took Angelina and gave her to Susannah.

"The president says you're very brave. He has decided to let you and your daughter go. He wants you to find the army that Sam Houston is raising. Go and tell them what happened here. Tell them that if they want to fight Santa Anna, they will be killed too. They cannot beat our army. We're too strong. Tell them if they want to live, they need to leave Texas and never come back."

Susannah looked at the general. "Thank you for helping me. I'll tell Sam Houston and his army what happened here. I think when they hear my story they won't leave Texas. They'll be so mad that they'll find your army and send you back to Mexico."

The general took Susannah's arm. "Come with me."

They walked out of the house. As they walked outside Susannah saw Ana Esparza walking into the house with her children. The two women looked at each other. They smiled, and then Susannah walked away with the general. We walked over to a soldier who was holding a small horse.

"Here is a horse for you. The president wants me to

give you two dollars and a blanket. We have heard that Sam Houston is in Gonzales. Just follow that road. You should be in Gonzales in a few days."

Susannah climbed onto the horse. She held Angelina and me on her lap.

"General, how did you know I was in the Alamo? When the officer came into our room he asked for me."

"You still have friends in San Antonio. One of them told us you were in the Alamo. I'm glad you weren't hurt."

"Thank you, General. You've been nice to me. I hope when Sam Houston's army catches you, you're not hurt and you can go home to your family."

The general stepped back and saluted Susannah. "I look forward to going home. I hope you have a safe trip."

Susannah nudged the horse forward. We rode slowly out of San Antonio. From where I was lying, I could see the enemy soldiers at the Alamo carrying the bodies of the Texans out of the Alamo and piling them up. Susannah saw them too and she gasped as she realized that they would be burned.

The horse slowly carried us toward Gonzales and the waiting Texan army. I was afraid that Santa Anna would change his mind and send his soldiers after us. I listened for the sound of horses running after us, but all I heard was the sound of our horse's hooves on the hard dirt road.

I knew that a thousand thoughts were going through Susannah's mind as we rode along. Thoughts of the long-ago days in Tennessee. Thoughts of coming to Texas and the happy times we had had before the war began. Finally, I knew she was thinking about the days in the Alamo. There had been some happy times. Some days of hope that more men would come to join us. But I think she was remembering the last hours and the terrible battle that had taken place. I could still hear the sound of the guns and hear the shouts of the men and smell the smoke from the cannons. I'll remember them all my life. I'll remember Colonel Travis and the ring he gave to Angelina. I'll remember Jim Bowie and his famous knife. I'll remember Davy Crockett and his fiddle and the jokes he told. I'll remember Ana Esparza and her children and the other women who shared our small room with us. I'll remember Almeron and the happy times we had. I'll remember all that, but most of all, I'll remember the Alamo.

Chapter Twenty-Six

THE TOYS STOOD LOOKING AT PATTY. The only sound was made by her rocking chair as she slowly rocked back and forth. Finally the ballerina doll looked around.

"No matter how many times I hear that story," she said, "I cry every time."

She heard some sniffling behind her. She turned around and saw the tin soldier wiping his eyes.

"Why, soldier, are you crying?" she asked.

The soldier turned his head. "No, I'm not. I got some dust in my eye. This attic is so dusty it gets in my eyes and nose. I certainly wouldn't cry."

Patty smiled at the soldier. "I know. Sometimes I just get covered with dust. I think you are a very brave soldier. I know that if you were at the Alamo, you would have been as brave as anyone there."

"Do you really think so?" the soldier asked.

"Yes I do," Patty said. "Those men were brave because they were fighting for something they believed in. Susannah and the women were brave because they believed in what the men were fighting for."

The rocking horse moved over to the soldier. "I think you are brave too. I'll let you ride on me if you want to. I won't throw you off."

The soldier looked at Patty. "Thank you for telling us the story. I know you must miss Susannah very much."

Patty looked over the heads of the toys standing there. "Yes, I do. She was a very special friend. We had many good times together. She always took me with her. I miss her a lot."

"What's that?" someone asked.

The toys listened. They heard the grandfather clock downstairs begin to chime. The toys counted the chimes.

"It's six o'clock," someone said.

The toys looked at the window. A ray of sunlight came through the glass.

"Quick," the ballerina said. "It's morning. Get back to your places."

The toys hurried to their places. The ballerina turned to Patty. "I'll see you tonight, Patty."

Patty smiled. "Yes. Tonight we'll talk some more."

Patty watched the ballerina walk to her place. Soon all the toys were still. Patty listened to the sounds coming up from below. People were walking around. She heard the sound of voices. A child laughed. Soon the smell of breakfast cooking drifted up to the attic.

Patty listened to the sounds and smelled the food and remembered that long ago day when she had sat in another room and listened to the sound of guns firing, men yelling and women and children crying and praying. The smell then was of gunpowder filling the people's nostrils and burning their eyes. It was so long ago, but it seemed like only yesterday. She looked into the dim light of the attic and saw Susannah's face smiling at her. Patty smiled back.

"Good-bye, Susannah, my good friend," she said.

The sunlight began to fill the attic. Downstairs the house was full of life and the sounds of happy people getting ready to live a new day. Up in the attic, all was quiet and still.

THE END